MW00459705

BIODYNAMIC GREENHOUSE MANAGEMENT

by
Heinz Grotzke

with a preface by
PROF. H. H. KOEPF

Bio-Dynamic Farming
and Gardening Association, Inc.
25844 Butler Rd Junction City, OR 97448
U. S. A

1998

© Biodynamic Literature 1990, 1998

The following chapters have appeared previously in issues of *Biodynamics:*

Chapter 1	Fall 1966 ©
Chapters 2 & 3	Summer 1978 ©
Chapter 4	Spring 1980 ©
Chapter 5	Spring 1981 ©
Chapter 13	Spring 1964 ©

ISBN 0-938250-25-6
Printed in U.S.A.

Illustrations by MARIA MOTCH
Typesetting by MARILYN McDONALD
Cover by ROB DECKER

All rights reserved. No part of this publication may be reproduced, stored in a retrieval system, or transmitted, in any form or by any means, electronic, mechanical, photocopying, recording or otherwise, without the prior permission of the publishers.

Contents

Preface

This book springs from a life of successful gardening in the greenhouse and in the field. Everything in the book is born from an in-depth understanding of plant life that Heinz Grotzke has assembled in his work as a professional gardener. In this work he is guided and motivated by the biodynamic approach that was put forward by Rudolf Steiner. The content is presented in the straightforward language that can only be achieved by a long-standing familiarity with the work.

Although the book includes a terrific amount of specific and useful advice, it is not just dry technical instructions. Each topic, i.e., choosing a type of greenhouse, soils, water, air, light, temperature, crop management, and so on, is discussed out of the individual spiritual search of the author into the working of living nature. The reader will find a stimulus for his or her own path to the skills and ethics of the vocation.

From the mid-1960s until recently, Heinz Grotzke built up and ran Meadowbrook Herb Garden in Wyoming, Rhode Island. He grew herbs for retail and wholesale distribution and had facilities for making herb teas and other mixtures. Each visit to the place was a great pleasure for the eyes and nose; utmost care for quality, and attention to the detail were the distinguishing marks of the soil cultivation, composting, biodynamic treatment, harvesting, and processing. His personal devotion to the task, that also speaks so strongly in this book, could be felt throughout the whole operation.

Since the mid-1950s, when Ehrenfried Pfeiffer was still leading the biodynamic movement in this country, Heinz has served on the Board of Directors of the Bio-Dynamic Farming and Gardening Association, Inc. From 1968 until 1984 he was the editor of "Biodynamics," the journal of the movement, and for many years he carried the work as Executive Director and Treasurer of the Bio-Dynamic Association. These many contributions reveal the kind of responsibility towards the cause that can also be experienced in this presentation.

I am confident that professional and private greenhouse gardeners will find sound advice and a stimulating depth of insight in this publication.

> Herbert H. Koepf
> Dr. Agr.
> Head of School of Biodynamic Agriculture
> Emerson College, England

Introduction

In the following pages the attempt has been made to simultaneously address two specific subject areas: greenhouse management and biodynamic concepts and practices. Greenhouse management is the primary topic. The biodynamic philosophy, terminology and method, by necessity, is only touched upon at certain points whenever this seems to add to the clarity of the presentation. But in general, it must be assumed that the reader either has acquired already a basic understanding of biodynamics, or might become interested enough to do so.

In my own mind I formulate, or define, biodynamics as the attempt to renew agriculture and horticulture through spiritual science, through Anthroposophy. Rudolf Steiner and other pioneering farmers and gardeners, who established the biodynamic approach to nature during the past sixty-five years, accumulated a range of specific terms which might be considered vague to the uninitiated reader. And yet most of them were used throughout the centuries by mystics, natural scientists, even philosophers and physicians, like Paracelsus for example. Nature forces and elemental beings are no discovery of our century; they

1

have been realities ever since the human being began to inhabit the earth. The human mind has been on a voyage of discovery from the first moment of creation and will continue to learn each and every day. The diversity between us all is merely a difference in acquiring knowledge in time. The first chapters of this book have appeared earlier in the quarterly magazine BIODYNAMICS.* They still seemed valid to this day and were left intact. The original impulse to write a book on gardening, including greenhouse management, was given to me by Dr. Ehrenfried Pfeiffer who suggested to publish the material in sections. He in fact thought it even possible at the time to begin a correspondence course on biodynamics. The only factor which delayed the whole progress was a constant lack of time.

The material presented here is based on personal experience alone and is certainly not always objective. The practical aspects, however, are attempted to be given in a precise and detailed manner, limited by my personal understanding alone. In concluding, I wish to point out that there is no substitute for formal training over a period of time, including greenhouse management. This statement, possibly more than any other, is strongly underscored by personal experience.

Fall 1989

Heinz Grotzke

---

*The Journal of the Bio-Dynamic Farming & Gardening Association, Inc., Kimberton, PA, published since 1941.

CHAPTER 1

An Overview

The first decision a prospective greenhouse grower has to make is in choosing the type of greenhouse he or she wants to own. There are two fundamental types: the free-standing greenhouse and the attached greenhouse. The first is an independent glass house, set apart from other buildings, with a door at one or both ends. The attached greenhouse can be either a Lean-to for side connection, or an Even Span for end connection. Both of these latter types are favorites among many home gardeners because their connection to another building makes them accessible from indoors, easy to heat, and generally lower in cost, since an existing building provides one side or end.

Each type of greenhouse has its advantages. A Lean-to is priced lower and needs less space, while an Even Span offers up to 50% more growing space at small added cost and can be built in any length at right angles to another building. It also is easier to cool and ventilate in summer. For the particular details of heating and construction materials, it is advisable to consult a greenhouse manufacturer. Often the greenhouse can easily be connected to the heating system of the home.

Nearly all plants can be grown successfully indoors when the harsh weather outside brings growth to a halt. The growing period of plants under glass can be extended to suit all and every person and reason, including the mere fun or plain interest in growing plants all year round. Many people already experience the constant companionship of their house plants throughout the year, yet unfortunately not all of those plants thrive on a window sill or on the cool porch, as many people undoubtedly have found out. Quite often, when selling potted plants and when talking to customers, I hear the earnest expression, "I wish I had a greenhouse!" And actually more and more people are investing in small greenhouses of one sort or another. There is no doubt that everybody who loves plants will enjoy life so much more if he can surround himself with green and colorful growth in winter too, when the white snow creates such a lovely contrast.

Aside from gathering experience while gardening for fun, many other things, from within the greenhouse panes, will be observed and noted, often for the first time in one's life. One will be surprised, for example, to feel the underestimated power of the sun which alone, on a frosty winter day, heats the whole greenhouse. Then too, it will be fascinating to study the beautiful ice patterns which form on the inside of the glass and which vary so surprisingly with the particular plant that inspired the artful design. Odors and escaping oils must be responsible for these bizarre drawings. Of course, observations like these are an extra bonus for the curious and observant mind and perhaps of little

4

aid to the beginning greenhouse gardener who, above all, is anxious to discover the secrets of successful growing under glass, provided there are such secrets. After becoming more familiar with the subject, the reader may decide for himself.

A greenhouse-grown plant should be exposed *gradually* to the outside world, to the forces of wind and weather, of sun and rain, so that it can continue growing without being subjected to a shock treatment. Every expert tries to avoid the latter and calls this gradual adjustment "hardening-off." The beginning greenhouse gardener, to be sure, has to undergo the same procedure, only in reverse: he has to be "softened-off," he has to be adjusted gently to the conditions under glass, and this merely in order to spare him a possible shock which could result from sudden awakening and change.

What then is so different in greenhouse growing compared to our outside gardening recreation? Above all it is the climate which differs greatly from the outdoor conditions. It is quite artificial since warmth, water, and air are completely controlled. A greenhouse creates a microclimate inside, following, it is true, the rhythm of day and night, but otherwise being fully dependent upon the direction of the grower. Warmth is regulated by heating and ventilation; water is supplied through the hose alone; ventilation, i.e. the controlled access of outside air, determines the air circulation; and the growth of plants is supported or checked by one or all of the other factors.

Being able to control the climate, the greenhouse gardener is in a position to grow *almost any kind of plant at any time of the year.* The light requirement of plants, however, is the limiting factor, and must be taken into ac-

count. In midwinter the days are short; even in a greenhouse it is dark at five in the afternoon. Some plants, like
tomatoes or cucumbers, simply go on strike during those
short days and long nights. It is light they need and wait
for; and if it is unavailable, the plants become diseased and
are a sorry sight.

Temperature is closely related to the light conditions in
a greenhouse. The shorter the days and the cloudier the
skies, the lower the temperature in the house should be
kept. Light and warmth regulate the growth of plants and
should always correspond to each other. The outside climate can teach us this lesson. The cold of winter arrives
when the days are short, whereas tiring heat hangs in the
bright summer sky. In many instances such a reference to
the natural outdoor climate proves quite helpful. In general, it is healthier for plants to keep the temperature in
a greenhouse rather a bit too low than too high.

The water needs of greenhouse plants have to be filled
through the rubber hose or watering can. The handling of
watering is perhaps the most decisive single factor which
determines the success or failure of greenhouse growing.
Until a person has acquired an instinctive feeling for it,
pots should be checked again and again in order to see
whether the right amount of water has been furnished.
The detailed technique will be discussed in a second part,
together with other practical aspects of greenhouse gardening. In the present discussion it is, however, necessary to
emphasize the fact that water in the greenhouse not only
fills the water requirements of plants, but also controls the
humidity of the air.

The humidity in turn determines the evaporation and
drying out of soil and pots. Furthermore, the humidity, pro-

perly controlled, helps to check insect infestations — especially of aphids — and diseases. It is true, different plants thrive under different concentrations of humidity, but here it is assumed that the greenhouse boards a variety of plants which thus require a happy medium. In summary, the general rule is to water sparingly rather than pouring on too much. A plant will show its need for water by wilting, yet it will flourish again after a drink; if, on the other hand, it starts to wilt because the roots, due to excessive moisture, have begun to rot, then little can be done. As for humidity, keep it high on warm, sunny days, and low during the night and on cloudy days.

Ventilation is provided by turning a crank which opens windows at an angle, or as some up-to-date houses are arranged, *one only sets a thermostat!* Temperature and air circulation are regulated by ventilation, at times also humidity. The effectiveness of ventilation is determined by the type of greenhouse. All houses have top ventilation, some the whole length, others partly. Side ventilation is available, though not always made use of. In deciding for one or the other type of ventilation, the decisive factor actually is what the greenhouse gardener wants to grow. An all-purpose house and one with benches hardly needs side ventilation, while a house for tomatoes, for example, should have it. A crop like this is usually grown not on benches but in the actual soil of the house. In recent years many growers employ electric fans to increase the air circulation in the greenhouse. Problems of mildew and other diseases are said to be reduced; some even claim that insects like white flies are held in check. Ventilation is an important part of greenhouse management and very seldom can be overused. In brief, it is better to ventilate than to retain too much old air.

After discussing the artificial microclimate with all its parts, let us turn to the light requirements. I remember this subject well, for almost twenty years now. "Light is the element of life!" was the favorite expression of my first teacher in horticulture whenever light fell on us. What he actually meant to say to us greenhorns was to scrub the window panes a little longer. At that time I had different feelings about this matter and thought, "How much can you exaggerate!" However, as years passed by, thoughts and feelings of that nature vanished and left the light behind, that light which is the element of life. There is a great deal of truth in it, as I found out myself.

It is impossible to put too much emphasis on the importance of clean windows. Especially the inside formations of algae, rotten or dried leaves, and other foreign matter should be washed off regularly. Rain and snow will keep the outside fairly clean; the glass along the sides though might need an occasional cleaning here and there. Glass in itself filters out a high percentage of ultraviolet rays, and all accumulated foreign matter on the glass ought to be removed in order to get the whole benefit of the sunlight. Shading in summer is a totally different story. It is a means of holding the temperature down rather than creating ideal growing conditions.

With this, the first chapter comes to an end. The techniques of the various phases of practical growing will be discussed in the following pages.

CHAPTER 2

Primary Considerations

In approaching greenhouse gardening from a purely bio-dynamic point of view, it is especially helpful for us to analyze quite clearly the essential factors and components involved.

The intent of a greenhouse grower is to give shelter to plants. The plants are basically meant to be protected from cold, though many times additional heat is supplied to create a temperature range within which the plants are accustomed to thrive. In doing this, we alter the natural growing condition of the plants and take them out of all their close connections to the forces and cycles of nature except for the continuing influence of day and night. One of the main growth requirements, however — the rain — is kept out and must be replaced by other means.

After these brief references it is easy to recognize that a greenhouse creates an artificial environment for the plants which are grown in it. Whatever we supply in the form of heat, water, light and soil is a mere substitute and

9

should be seen as such. It follows that plants grown in greenhouses cannot be a match for those which grow under the eye of the sun and among the elements of nature. On the other hand, a greenhouse provides the only way in which we can enjoy all the plants which are native to the southern parts of the world, like orchids, tender vegetables and flowers.

Keeping these thoughts in mind, it will be easier to define the goals which we set ourselves as practicing growers. Our attempts should be adjusted to fall within the realm of the possible, especially if we use a greenhouse as a source of income. Each crop has a growing range in time within which it will be possible to nurture it, without resorting to ultramodern techniques and costs exceeding market value.

The methods employed in growing a plant are generally based upon the understanding or concept of what the plant is, and what its intended use will be. Biodynamic ideas about plants differ basically from the orthodox scientific premises; consequently, biodynamic greenhouse growing must vary in many respects from what might be called common greenhouse practice.

A definition of the plant, in biodynamic terms, may be explained on several levels. The most important characteristics are worth mentioning for the sake of clarity.

Seen within the evolutionary process of the world, the plant is a living entity existing between the mineral, or material, substance of the earth on one side, and the multitude of animals on the other. The mineral is absorbed and taken up into the plant; the animal, while following the plant in evolution, entirely depends on it. Within this image, the plant has a central position as the first being to carry life.

As such, the plant unfolds its substantiality between the earth and the heavens, or cosmos. It needs both to exist: substance from the earth and life from the cosmos. The sun as sole life source makes each plant a child of the sun, rooted in the soil, conveying and giving life forces to all that inhabit the earth.

Armed with these definitions of the plant we will have enough respect and understanding to acknowledge the need of the plant to remain earth-bound, even in the greenhouse growing, and hydroponic methods need never be considered; not even soil-less "soil" has found any justification in biodynamic circles. A healthy plant needs the soil as much as it needs the sun. The assumption that the growing medium, to use a professional term, can be any material as long as it holds water, nutrients and roots is not accepted by biodynamic growers. The plant roots can well distinguish between different types of substances; the great variations of root growth and formation can easily be observed in studying soil-type in relation to root behavior of one and the same plant species. In the greenhouse, the emphasis on soil life activity also holds true, regardless of whether the soil is in pot or flat or is the actual greenhouse ground.

The specific aids for biodynamic crop production are certainly made part of any greenhouse operation, rather more intensely than in outdoor areas simply because we deal with a more artificial environment and must attempt to overcome some of its weaknesses. This subject will be given more detailed treatment later, *after* a discussion of the very basic management skills.

11

CHAPTER 3

Sanitation

In addressing groups of people about biodynamic greenhouse practices, I am often asked what sequence of importance I would attach to routine greenhouse management chores. I, in my own mind, have determined such a sequence, even though it might be subjective and not entirely applicable to someone else. Still, I can look back on nearly forty years of greenhouse experience, most of it under biodynamic management. So I simply will discuss these points as they seem important to me, realizing that some readers might change the order.

When I bring this issue up before an audience, people never even guess what area I would emphasize first. But in a biodynamic greenhouse the greatest awareness should be placed on, and utmost efforts directed toward, sanitation. Growers who have actual greenhouse experience will understand the reasons behind this statement more easily than beginners; the fact that we are discussing *biodynamic* management makes no difference here.

The greenhouse environment is created by the grower, who becomes the guardian of the plants and at the same time takes over the responsibilities of Mother Nature. The plants are given shelter, water, nutrients, warmth, and provision for light. *How* this is done reflects the inner convictions and qualities of the grower. The forest, the mountain meadow, or the hidden pond can exist without the human being, but a greenhouse cannot. Being aware of this great difference, we can easily understand that the relationship between the grower and the plant is more intimate and rewarding here than anywhere else where plants are grown; at least from a biodynamic point of view, it should be.

Once an inkling of understanding penetrates one's mind, little surprise will accompany the revelation that the natural environment of the plant world is clean. Must I remind you of the beauty and innocence of an opening rose, the blinking pearl of dew on a leaf of lady's mantle in the early morning hours? Wherever we look, plants abound with beauty, created by purity of substances. Even the dark of the forest floor resembles a carpet woven by artisans with meticulous care.

How do plants keep themselves and their environment so clean? Even the fallen pine needles do not offend the eye, nor does the whitening milkweed when it bids farewell to its offspring in serene beauty. There is no sorrow when the life of a plant has been fulfilled; the remains are accepted by the wisdom of nature and transformed into another form, for another purpose.

In the greenhouse, the grower has to provide the same wisdom that brings about a sense of beauty and reflects cleanliness and order throughout all seasons. He owes it to the captured plants, and they expect it of him. This is only one aspect of sanitation (perhaps considered by some as too ideal and subtle), but it is as real and as important as the following one, in which logical and abstract thinking become valid.

Adopting and practicing sanitary habits in a greenhouse means recognizing that a greenhouse is the opposite of a composting area. A greenhouse environment has been established with great effort for one purpose: to grow and cultivate desirable plants. Growing is the opposite of decaying. It becomes mere logic to eliminate by all means possible sources initiating and generating any form of decomposition. All our aims and efforts are concentrated on the propagation of vegetables, flowers, or possibly herbs, but under no circumstances would we consider multiplying algae, fungi or bacteria. And yet, the latter is often easier to do than the first, unless the grower applies wisdom and will.

In practical terms, this means that the whole interior of the greenhouse has to be kept clean from debris and things that do not belong there. The area under the bench is not to be considered a dump; instead, it should appear well-tended and orderly if used for storage of non-decayable things like pots or flats. There is no objection to growing a ground cover of some sort as long as it is cared for. Dead plant material, like leaves or rotten fruit, should regularly be picked up and sent to the compost pile outside. The benches themselves, if wood, need regular treatment with a wood preservative like copper naphtanate, especially formulated for greenhouse purpose. Decaying wood can harbor and become host to fungi, which are not desirable.

Should the benches be filled with soil for growing crops

like lettuce, radish, kohlrabi, etc., then the soil requires the same cultivation which we offer our crops outside. Hoeing is very important, because the constant watering with a hose compacts the soil much more than does the gentle rain outside. All leaves of the growing plants, which for some reason turn yellow or show decay, should be broken off and discarded. Slugs might otherwise feel obligated to do this for you and, lacking sufficient supply, would have few scruples about feasting on the green leaves as well.

Pots on bench in sand

In case the benches are used for potted plants, the customary practice is to fill the benches with about two inches of sand for proper positioning of the pots. Again, this sand has to be and remain clean; no dirt or soil should be mixed with it. Continuous watering will, in time, compact the sand and develop at the top the formation of algae, aided occasionally by soil which spills over the pot rims during watering. In order to avoid this, it makes sense to pot the plants a fraction of an inch below the rim. The green algae coating of the sand is not desirable and needs routinely to be removed. At the same time the sand itself is loosened and given thereby a fresh appearance. The potted plants in such an area should also be lifted, protruding roots at the bottom cut off and the plant itself cleaned of dead leaves or yellowed sections. Should the roots already have taken hold in the sand, then those roots need to be removed from the sand before the pot is placed back on the bench. The all-pervading rule is to leave nothing in the greenhouse that is not a living plant!

The potted plants themselves need care. The soil surface in pots compacts from watering and tends to develop algae or moss just like the sand on the bench. Monthly hoeing of the pots with a small hoe, made from number 12 wire, is the best prevention and at the same time will promote healthy growth. Should time not permit this, or if the pots are simply neglected, then it eventually becomes necessary to scrape off the green layer on top of the soil. The exposed soil underneath is thereafter gently hoed and the pot filled with fresh soil to protect the exposed roots. The scrapings are destined for the compost, but in general this method is too much effort and too costly for the gathering of compost material!

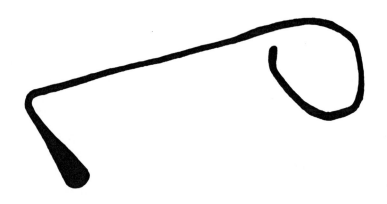

Little hoe for pots, made from 12-gauge wire

Once all these tasks of clean-up have been completed, the final glance is saved to check the windows. Even here the algae like to conquer territory and climb up from the corner. If they cannot be flushed down with a hose, then a sponge or cloth might do the trick. Under no circumstances should they be allowed to gain a permanent foothold. The adjoining wood or metal frame might be the starting point unless it is kept in good paint.

I hope my definition of sanitation in the greenhouse has become clear to everyone, even though a leaf or two might have been left unturned. The emphasis, from a bio-dynamic point of view, is on eliminating all possible sources of plant disease and bacterial infestation. Lifeless organic materials do not belong in a greenhouse; their place of resurrection is the compost pile.

CHAPTER 4

Soils

The soil for greenhouse crops is the most important factor determining performance, health and yields of the specific plant species to be propagated for hobby or income. Neither hydroponic culture nor soil-less "soil" blends would be considered by a biodynamic grower as growing media. In brief, hydroponic culture or artificial soils are as foreign to the plant being as are chemical fertilizers and insecticides.

The substance which we as farmers and gardeners handle as soil is a very complex medium and varies from place to place. We all have experienced the diversity of soil structure, soil behavior and soil performance. The present stage of our soil is the result of physical, biological and meteorological changes caused by forces which acted upon the original rock formation and biosphere over a long period of time. Still, certain elements, characteristics and properties will be found in all soil types, because without them vegetation would not be able to develop. Air in the form of wind, and water in the form of rain or flood, help to balance extremes and often make the first growth of plants possible.

Who of us has not seen moss on roof tiles, or tree seedlings which attempt to grow in the gutter, using leaves as soil substitutes? In simple terms, soil is a blend of inorganic and organic particles of various size. Determination of the inorganic portion by elements, and of the organic portion by its volume, ratio and degree of decomposition, identify the soil further and, in scientific terms, make the potential for supporting plant growth more predictable.

In biodynamic terms, soil is not seen quite so simply, although even here basic common denominators can be applied. Each soil is above all of siliceous nature; it harbors the element silicon which, when paired with oxygen in the form of silica, is commonly known as quartz. Our soils contain varying amounts of this substance; sandy soils are high in silica, heavy soils are low in it. The opposite, or polar, substance to silica is silt, the finest particles of which, in combination with other molecules, form clay in a soil. A third, somewhat mediating substance is lime, consisting of the element calcium, once again in union with oxygen. Reference may be made here to Rudolf Steiner's second lecture on agriculture.* The characters and functions of these soil representatives are described there, and their relationship to earth and cosmos is emphasized. In the following I will attempt to elaborate on the principles

---

*R. Steiner, *"Agriculture,"* (Bio-Dynamic Agriculture Association 1974)

outlined in the lecture and to apply them to greenhouse soil.

A greenhouse, especially if used for the commercial growing of pot plants, requires large amounts of soil each year. The problem of soil supply is solved by each grower in one way or the other, but generally the soil is simply trucked in by those who offer it for sale. In many cases it comes from industrial or housing developments where the top soil is sold off for purposes of establishing a lawn somewhere else, or, as in our case, sold to a greenhouse grower who will sterilize it, add fertilizer and possibly peat and/or vermiculite to fit his formula. Soil handled in this way is considered a natural resource and is marketable as long as it is available.

Wishing to avoid harming the earth organism, the biodynamic grower will seldom participate in robbing soil from another area where it belongs. He will instead manufacture soil for the greenhouse through the familiar composting process. In this way all greenhouse soil will be virgin soil, a blend of various composts with additions of sand or crushed granite, particularly formulated to support the crop that is to be grown.

Since greenhouse soil is a man-made soil, we are able to define our goals and take steps to reach them. What do we expect of a greenhouse soil? The fertilizing properties of the soil have to be more concentrated than for a garden soil. The drainage condition has to allow for a fast and even penetration of water. The water-holding capacity has to be higher than in a garden soil. The structure of the soil has to guarantee ample and lasting aeration. The soil has to resemble and hold the characteristics of a natural soil and harbor those substances of earthly and cosmic nature which enable a healthy plant life to unfold. How can we meet all these criteria and achieve the proper greenhouse soil?

Composting becomes the productive tool and key for successful greenhouse production. It should be emphasized, however, that the methods of handling these composts differ from the methods used for farm composting. For reliable performance, a greenhouse soil must be consistent from year to year. As in many other areas of science, the only way to achieve consistency is to eliminate as many variables as possible. In practice this means that the raw materials for composting should be the same from year to year and should be composted separately. In our growing operation we have, basically, two composting processes going on side by side: we compost pure cow manure itself, and we compost weeds and plant residues, with the addition of some kitchen garbage; in other words, we compost animal substance and plant substance separately.

In Steiner's "Agriculture" lectures he also makes a distinction between these two types of composts. The plant compost contains nutrients plus an inherent vitality or *etheric** element. The cow manure has the nutrients, the etheric, and the added possibility to impart a sensitiveness, or *astrality** to the compost.

I fully realize that other animal manures would be suitable, but even with separate piles of cow manure and horse manure, we would already have three variables instead of

*For a more complete description of these terms, refer to "The Biodynamic Farm," H.H. Koepf (Anthroposophic Press, N.Y., 1989)

21

two. If different manures should be available, then for greenhouse use each manure should be composted by itself and blended, after completion, in uniform proportions year after year.

As I have pointed out, we use two types of compost materials: cow manure and plant refuse, mainly weeds. Since the organic raw materials, whether manure or weeds, have to be completely digested in the composting process, it takes in our northern climate a minimum of two years to reach the desired compost condition, and this not without turning the compost at least twice a year.* But then the compost looks, smells and behaves like the best humus soil, which in fact it is. These finished composts finally become the source for the greenhouse soil blend.

The finished cow manure and weed composts are blended in equal parts. What do we achieve, in bio-dynamic terms, with this action? The animal manure (and the less straw or bedding mixed with it, the better) retains a residue of astrality which, in the course of composting, is transformed into a new form of astrality. This slow and "cold" composting creates the ideal breeding place for the so-called compost worms (Eisenia foetida) which in reality digest the manure from the outside in and turn the pile into a heap of castings. The direction of the whole process, explained in terms of astrality, runs from what might be called a volatile state to a stable one. And silt plays an important role in this process, the same silt that Rudolf Steiner relates to the "near" planets, those planets near

---

*See "Compost, What It Is, What It Does, and How It Is Made," H.H. Koepf (Bio-Dynamic Association, 1980)

to the earth. The created humus, the captured astrality, is of earthly nature, is in fact as earthy as nature can produce it.

Although the weed compost has a different character, it also accumulates the earthy element. The starting point of the whole process, however, is a different one. What we disrespectfully call "weeds" are, in most cases, plants in their immature stage, prior to seeding, which are mostly a mass of leaves. It might not be done in practice for economical reasons, but if at least in our imagination we could compost the different parts of the plant separately, what would we find? Has anyone made a compost of flowers alone? Have you tried to compost nothing but roots? How about seeds? Each of these composts would have a different quality, would in fact be of different structure and color. And the relationship to earth astrality would be different.

By necessity and tradition we compost the leaf part, we compost weeds, and knowingly or not for a good reason. The leaf is the plant in its prime, is all plant; Goethe, through his intuition, saw nothing but leaves when he looked at plants.* Describing the leaves on the same level as when I referred to astrality, I would say that the leaf is all etheric. When we pull weeds in their young stage we pull ethericity, but bring to a halt at the same time a growth process that because of our action cannot be brought to an end. Instead, the weeds find their way

---

*"The Metamorphosis of Plants," Goethe (Bio-Dynamic Association, 1978). "Readings in Goethean Science," Koepf & Jolly (Bio-Dynamic Association 1978)

23

to the compost pile as a bunch of leaves, unable to fulfill the potential of reproduction. With the weeds we also compost that potential and achieve a finished product that, through its former leaf nature, is best able to support future leaf growth in our crops. Throughout this whole process, however, we remain in the realm of etheric forces, though earthbound.

The striking differences and similarities between the processes of cow manure composting and weed composting become clear when we also realize that the cow's main food is the leaf part of the plant in the form of grass, clover, hay or silage, and that, through her digestion, she initiates a sort of composting process, inside her living organism, that finally results in a benefit for soil fertility. Cow manure could be defined as an enlivened leaf compost which, by its own course within nature, supports soil life and soil fertility in the end. Even beyond this, a continuing composting process, with the aid of the earthworm, further refines humus quality and longevity.

By blending equal parts of cow manure compost and weed compost, we strengthen the earth forces in our future greenhouse soil and do so on a broad base. Qualities of animal astrality and of plant ethericity have been unified in the final product. The connection to the cosmic realms is still absent, however; the far planets do not yet find a receptive element. He who knows Steiner's lectures on agriculture will realize that silica is missing. The best additive to the soil blend would be granite crushed to the size of river sand or somewhat larger. For root growth the particle shape is an important factor. A crushed and screened rock, in our case granite, has sharp, pointed and irregular edges, a physical advantage for both drainage and (partly for the same reason) root formation, especially the development of secondary roots as they occur on cuttings and young seedlings.

A further advantage of crushed granite, as compared, for example, to river sand, is difficult to explain in common terms and more difficult, perhaps, to comprehend and accept, although a discussion of this issue lies entirely within the realm of biodynamic thinking. In nature, over a period of thousands of years, rock size has been reduced through physical forces like weathering, motion, and temperature extremes, as well as through biological action. Our present accumulated soil is the final result, and the "crushing" process continues to work upon the surface of earth matter.

In applying this concept of rock disintegration, we view the single soil particle as a representative of a specific stage of aging. At each one of these progressions of aging, energies are released which were accumulated and concentrated in the rock when it originally was formed. It might be compared to a piece of wood which burns in the oven and, by burning, releases energy in the form of heat. Although the energy itself was captured by the wood on the earth, it originated from the sun. The rock in the process of disintegration does not release earthly heat of cosmic origin, but instead other forces are set free which, however, are as much of cosmic origin as the heat created by the burning of wood.

We do not sense these forces, but nature does. In their totality they become part of nature and act upon plant growth as nature or elemental forces. The slow pace of disintegration of rock, as it occurred for thousands of years in nature forming our soils, has released in the process a slow but constant supply of elemental forces which, in combination with biological systems, supported plant growth. The soil particle itself finally disintegrates to the point of dust just as, through fire, the wood turns to ashes.

From the standpoint of disintegration, the crushed granite for our greenhouse soil is far removed from dust; it is virgin compared to river sand, which, through tumbling along in river beds for thousands of years, has lost its "young edges."

For our soil we currently use sand that we find in our subsoil because this present location is blessed with clean sand, free of rocks and organic particles. Should the source of sand be unknown or questionable, it is best to wash the sand with clean water and flush out soluables and organic matter. This is also done for the purpose of having a uniform ingredient for our greenhouse soil. Screening might be necessary for the same reason if particle size varies.

Crushed granite or sand is finally blended with the other ingredients in one part to four parts each of composted cow manure and composted weeds. The soil thus created has all the ingredients of regular soil in a concentrated form and will bring about the desired plant growth. The blend is considered a standard potting and greenhouse soil and has been used in practical work for vegetable and herb crops for many years. The soil analysis for three years showed the figures for basic nutrients:

Potting Soil Analysis

	CEC	Organic Matter %	pH	NO₃-N	P₂O₅	K	Ca	Mg
				ppm				
1977	26.2	12.0	6.8	35	225	355	3000	1000
1978	29.2	13.2	6.6	20	125	390	4750	465
1979	20.7	8.4	6.7	25	510	255	2500	600

Specific crops might need a slight variation in pH, structure, aeration, or might call for other requirements. But it will always be possible to use the blend as a base to which other ingredients can be added. For example, lavender prefers a higher pH. All that needs to be done is add wood ashes to the volume of soil that is needed to pot lavender. Tomatoes need a more fertile and coarser consistency, so one third of one-year-old cow manure compost is added. Ferns prefer a medium with better water holding capacity and possibly lower pH, therefore shredded spaghnum moss could be added to about one half of the growing medium. There is no crop in the greenhouse that cannot be grown with the manufactured soil blend.

Possibilities of refinement should not be neglected, however. A well-proven ingredient for greenhouse soil is leaf compost, preferably from soft-wood leaves. For faster decomposition it is best to shred the leaves and then compost them until they become real earth. Comfrey leaves are sometimes available in abundance and turn, if composted, into precious soil. Spaghnum moss might be available in some areas and could be used for composting; where it is accessible, seaweed can be composted. Sometimes the availability of materials is surprising. But in all cases, provided of course sufficient quantities are available, these supplements should be composted separately and consistently added to the greenhouse soil for reliable performance.

In case a reader is not familiar with biodynamic concepts, it should be made clear that all references to composting are understood to include the use of the biodynamic compost preparations: nettle, dandelion, camomile, yarrow, oakbark and valerian. The definition of composting, especially for greenhouse use, also includes the necessity to arrive at a final product with a narrow range of particle size, resembling about the screened portion of a 1/8" mesh. For many years we have successfully used a Royer soil shredder and find little need for screening.

The question of lime, as it is related to composting, might need a brief clarification. Lime should never be added to the manure during the composting process. The accumulated weeds for composting will not need liming either, if the weeds dumped on the pile carry with them, around the roots, a fair amount of garden soil. If nothing but leaf mass is available, the first choice would be to add some old compost as the pile is being built; the second choice would be to sprinkle some ground limestone or quick lime in layers on the material. It must be realized that an aerobic decomposition — and we cannot allow any other — will create a final compost product which is higher in pH than that found in the raw materials. In case the blended greenhouse soil should prove to be too far away from a neutral hydrogen ion concentration (pH 7.0), adjustment should be made by adding screened wood ashes to the soil.

Some greenhouse growers who specialize in flowering plants, or even in a crop like tomatoes, might feel more comfortable if a higher phosphorus level could be reached. It then becomes advisable to add bone meal to the composting process, though not necessarily at the very beginning of the two-year composting cycle. One growing season will generally be sufficient to decompose the finely ground bone. At no time should mold, attached to the bone particle, still be detectable when the soil is brought into the greenhouse. All decomposition within the compost itself has to be completed before it is suitable for greenhouse use.

In order to completely cover all possible uses for greenhouse soil, I have to distinguish between three areas of use. The soil can be used to grow plants in pots; it can also be placed in a raised bench area where crops can be grown without pots; or it can be used for growing crops directly on the ground in the greenhouse soil itself, either not elevated at all or, possibly, confined somewhat in beds. Soil handling is different for each of these areas.

The entire discussion of greenhouse soil up to this point has described the making of soil for potting. The soil thus created will prove ideal because of its nutrient balance, high absorption of water, good water-holding capacity and acceptance of warmth due to its dark color. The humus component is stable so that even after months the structure remains unchanged, enabling a continued good aeration in spite of almost daily watering. Proper root formation is dependent upon good aeration.

A great amount of work in the greenhouse is needed to shift plants from one size pot to another, and the behavior of the root ball determines to a degree the time required to do it, as well as the continued undisturbed growth of the plant in the new pot. The less the root ball is disturbed the better; ideally it should not fall apart. Whether or not it does, depends on the soil. The soil blend achieved by the above-mentioned methods will hold the ball, provided uniform moisture content exists, a condition which should always be present. A simple check can be made by unpotting one plant. The soil should be of even dark color. Compare this blend with others that you may encounter when, for example, you buy petunias which drop all the soil from their roots when you unpot them.

Many greenhouse crops — especially vegetables like lettuce, radishes, cucumbers and others — can be grown on benches, without pots. The height of the soil on the bench should be an average of 8 inches, which means that for a bench area of 100 square feet we need 67 cubic feet or 2½ cubic yards of soil. Our same greenhouse soil can be, or in fact should be, used for this type of culture. The filling of the benches is, however, done with some thought and the soil is not just dumped onto the benches.

When we study the natural formation of a soil profile outdoors, we will observe in most cases how the particle size becomes larger as we dig into the subsoil. In the greenhouse we imitate nature's proven method when filling the benches with soil. The soil intended for use is hand-screened with a ¼-inch wire screen and the screenings placed in the bench as the bottom layer. Depending on the soil mixture, the accumulation of screenings will vary, determining the thickness of this bottom layer. However, this is of no crucial importance since the major intent is to separate somewhat the available soil. Just by screening a portion, we are able to achieve three types: 1) the screenings, 2) the screened soil, 3) the original soil. The eight inches of soil in the bench can, for example, be reached by using one inch of screenings for a bottom layer, five inches of unscreened soil as the medium layer, and two inches of screened soil as the top layer. The actual proportions will necessarily vary with each available greenhouse soil.

Profile of Bench Soil

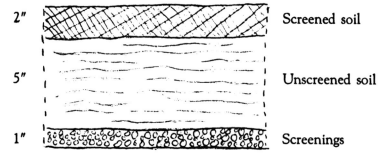

An advantage of this type of soil building in the benches is an increased downward aeration capability and an increased downward water transfer capacity, all based on particle size. In many cases this arrangement will also correct the possible results of overwatering because the coarse portion of the bottom layer is able to harbor more excess water, preventing it from staying in the upper layers. A good check to avoid this type of inexperience can be made by placing a fine wire mesh tube vertically in the soil down to the bottom of the bench. The grower can then visually judge the "ground-water" conditions at any time. The top layer of screened soil will allow direct seedings of fine seeds without additional preparation.

Many commercial greenhouse crops — tomatoes, cauliflower, roses, carnations, for example — are grown directly in the greenhouse soil to allow for deep root penetration. Such soil may either be the same as that outside, meaning that the greenhouse was simply built over an area, or the soil may be specially prepared. But in no case would it be made up entirely of a compost blend such as we have been discussing. Our greenhouse soil will, however, also be suitable for this type of growing practice. It becomes the fertilizing medium which is spread over the growing area like any other compost that is used for biodynamic crop production. The rate of application is determined by the crop to be grown. The compost soil, composed according to the directions given earlier, is the proper fertilizer medium for such crops as lettuce, radishes, carrots, beans, onions, most herb crops, and flowers. A crop of tomatoes and cauliflower would need a "fresher" compost material, at the most one year old. Every addition of compost to the greenhouse soil should be worked into the soil with hoe, cultivator or rototiller.

Soil storage can be handled in several ways. The most common practice is to hold the different compost piles outside until portions are needed for soil blending. Outside storage in shade generally eliminates the problem of having the pile dry out entirely. Rainfall holds the moisture content uniform. The soil needs for winter and spring determine how much soil will be required to have potting soil available for potting early plants in January, February and March. In our operation, it has worked best if we mix the required soil in November/December and place the soil mix under the greenhouse benches. Temperature is cool, contact with the ground is retained, and water can easily be added when we water the greenhouse. Occasional weeding of germinating seeds might be necessary.

The subject of soil treatments must also be included in any discussion of greenhouse soils. In biodynamic work this issue is of minor importance because soil fumigants, soil sterilizing agents, and soil insecticides are not accepted tools of greenhouse management. The only practice which can be considered under the category of soil treatment would be soil steaming or soil heating. Both are used to destroy weed seeds or soil pathogens.

The steaming of compost soil in general would defeat the attempt to increase soil life activity. The steaming of soil with a high population of earthworms, in particular, does not make sense from a biodynamic point of view. However, this type of earthworm, the compost worm, should not leave the composting area in the first place. Even compost for garden or field should be low in earthworm population because the worms will not survive garden conditions either.

The composts destined for greenhouse soil should be void of worms altogether. The worms retreat from a ripe, finished compost. Therefore, the steaming of greenhouse soil cannot be objectionable from that point of view. And yet the steaming should be seen only as a measure for eliminating the germination capability of weed seeds from soil that is used for the propagation of young seedlings. In my experience it has never seemed possible to have weed-free compost soil, though in theory there are many reasons why it should be possible to achieve such ideal compost.

The temperature necessary to destroy the germinating power of weed seeds is a minimum of 160°F. With thermostat setting, the cut-off should be 170°F and the cut-in 160°F. This temperature should be held for 30 minutes after the desired temperature has been reached. Steam-producing soil sterilizers are very expensive, so most people resort to electric soil heaters. But you can apply the principle of steaming here also by making sure that the soil moisture is high, especially around the heating elements, so that this excess moisture can turn into steam.

In summary, the biodynamic growing of greenhouse crops must put great emphasis on compost management for the production of the required volume of greenhouse soil. The composting process has to be brought to the final stage of complete decomposition of crude organic substance. Blending the various types with an additional, silica-rich mineral must be carried out in a precise manner in consistent proportions in order to achieve a reliable greenhouse soil of uniform and satisfactory performance. Proper attention must be given to soil storage aimed at keeping the medium alive and in contact with the earth. Soil treatment in biodynamic management is limited to the possible steaming of soil for the purpose of ridding the growing medium of weed seed viability.

CHAPTER 5
_____

Water

Water is such a magic word, harboring the promise of quenching the thirst of those who have ventured too close to the heat of ambition, of desire, of the burning bush. Water is further defined by a host of attributes which express a definite mood or experience: clear, cool, blue, refreshing, salty, calm, stormy — we have been acquainted with all these aspects of water for a long time. What waters does your soul recognize if you turn to your memory?

The water that enters my mind is one of the elements referred to by Aristotle. I admit that this might not be a precise definition for the kind of person who translates even the vastness of the oceans into numbers and formulas, but consider the manifold advantages of Aristotle's description: water as a state of existence, water as a substance with a hundred faces, water as the ultimate expression of fluidity, flowing without form, existing without vessel, escaping without being captured.

There are a thousand states of existence that could justly

be related to water, yet our discussion is meant to deal with the water of life and to reveal but one relationship: the role that water plays in greenhouse management. All other roles, as intriguing as they might be, will have to wait for exploration until some other occasion.

Nature, with all its objects and forces, remains a hidden secret most of the time; occasionally, however, it graciously passes on to man bits of information, although not necessarily in logical sequence. You may have some idea of what I mean, especially you old-timers who have knocked your heads against Mother Nature for a length of time, as I have. Each time this happens we adjust our insight a little bit, due to the unavoidable translocation of some rusted thoughts!

Prior to the last adjustment, I clung fast to the notion, implanted decades ago by the self-made career gardener who happened to be my imposing instructor, that light is the element of life, especially of plant life. Who would want to deny the validity of such a strong statement? Without light there would be no plant life, and possibly little other life as well. And yet, light the element of life?

Aristotle did not know this element at all, or at least did not find it appropriate to call light an element. Of the four elements, earth, water, air and fire, it is the air that has the closest relationship to light; in fact, Aristotle's element of air is best understood as light-filled air. The light of the sun penetrates and fills the air and creates it every day anew. When the light withdraws at night, a form of vacuum results which is filled by the light of the moon, the stars, or even by elemental forces which fear the light because it would mean danger, even death, to them. Creatures like moths and bats come to our minds.

In this darkness, I lost sight of what was happening in the greenhouse. I understood light to be the element of life, certainly in my former years of study, until I discovered another quality of water and modified my understanding of life with all its implications. It is definitely true that life on earth would not be possible without the constant inflow of light from the distant sun. We might call light the source and sustainer of life, the cosmic power which keeps the life burning until the carrier is consumed, is exhausted. What, then, is the carrier? It is water. Water is the carrier of life. An immense burden and responsibility is put upon this element, and we must recognize it, now and for the sake of the future. Water and life weave mysterious bonds of relationship, expressing levels of existence in constant change. A thousand faces stare at us. Before we have a chance to give each one a name, a different image confronts us.

After placing water on earth, in its true context within nature, and stressing how important it is for the existence and continuation of life, we are now prepared to consider the "profane" role which water plays in greenhouse management.

No matter what crop or culture a greenhouse is occupied with, it definitely will need water. Water sustains plant life and, in combination with light and warmth, determines the rate of plant growth. An analysis of any greenhouse crop would show that it consists predominently of water. The source of the water is the watering can, the hose, or the sprinkler, all governed by the grower, who decides at what time what amount of water will enter the greenhouse. He thus becomes the only and supreme commander of life and death over the greenhouse crops. The plants are inescapably dependent upon the one who controls the water. Fortunately for most plants in greenhouses, the grower desires to be a benevolent ruler and prides himself on lush, well-watered plants, especially if they are to be exchanged for coin or bill.

Unfortunately, the control of water in greenhouses, or the proper handling of it, is not an innate skill, but has to be developed over many years. In their youth, some prospective growers probably felt this concern of their elders to be over-emphasized, yet time proves to be an unforgiving teacher. Who has found, throughout the centuries, a meaningful way of disputing with time or of arguing forcefully in the presence of sad proof obvious to anyone who dares to look? Plants blessed with too much water, or those which do not remember any longer what water feels like, are a sad sight. Every greenhouse grower is determined to spare himself such a sight, though rarely will he be able to escape it.

Water is brought into the greenhouse to a) sustain growth, b) control humidity, and c) discourage the settling down of undesirable insects. All this has to be done, however, without encouraging the formation and spreading of fungus diseases. As in any human endeavor, success or failure are both possible, though they rarely occur at the same time. Generally, human progress is established by beginning with a great deal of error resulting in failure, and by gradually omitting mistakes until all the problems seem to be corrected. The absence of acts which can no longer foster failure is finally called success. Water management in greenhouses is no exception.

In this section I wish to answer all the questions that have been put to me over many years. Questions like,

"How long should I water?", "How many gallons of water should be used per bench?", "Should I stop for lunch or keep watering during my lunch hour?" The fountain of questions draws from a never-ending source, while the tower of answers will collapse before it reaches the sky.

The source of water, on the other hand, sometimes runs dry, especially if the greenhouse grower is dependent upon his own water supply. The summer of 1980 was a good example. A reliable water supply is a basic requirement for greenhouse growing. Plants are the most patient creatures on earth, by far surpassing our fellow man, but they have little understanding for human problems, even less for those which are connected to mechanical ingenuity, like water supply systems. The final analysis is simple: no water, no plants. Of course I realize that this statement will take no one by surprise, and yet the real meaning strikes home only when the greenhouse grower must, through circumstances, become a water carrier to save the plants' life and his own solvency. It then also becomes very clear that water is a flowing element, though with an unfortunate tendency to flow only downhill!

In some greenhouses the water comes from a public supply, especially for growers who live in urban communities and either practice greenhouse growing as a hobby or are florists. There is little objection to city water unless it is chlorinated or fluoridated. Both substances, chlorine and fluoride, will not support the biodynamic grower's efforts to increase soil life activity, and since this has a bearing on insect management in the greenhouse, an alternative water source is preferable. Filtering systems can provide a solution or, at least in the case of chlorination, a large vessel may be used for storing the water used in the greenhouse. Some means of circulation will even enhance the escape of chlorine, the more so if this is possible in sunlight.

The larger or commercial grower will probably have his own water supply system. The two common sources are either a dug well or an artesian well, the first more dominant in areas with a high ground-water level and the second in locations where water veins run deep. In either case it is important to have the water tested for pH, iron content and bacteria content and count, as well as for impurities or pollutants which under normal conditions are not considered part of water. The quality of water throughout the country has deteriorated at an astonishing rate during the last decades. Pollutants like nitrates, detergents, petroleum products, even pesticides are no rarity any longer.

For greenhouse use, the pH factor is of utmost importance. Depending upon the subsoil of the area, the water is either acid or alkaline, in some cases possibly neutral. The desirable pH is 7.0; in other words, it is the rare case that the grower is after. However, a range of the pH from 6.5 to 7.5 is acceptable. The neutral factor is desired because all crops grow best in a known range of soil pH which the greenhouse grower tries to maintain through cultural practices, soil mixes, etc. Should the water be other than neutral, a steady change of the hydrogen ion concentration (pH) would take place through watering, and a stable condition could never be achieved. This would become the more apparent the longer the crop was watered.

An accomplished grower has little choice but to neutralize his water, especially if it should be acid. This can be done by any water conditioning firm, and generally is a costly, though valuable investment.

The biodynamic grower must put more emphasis on the

pH factor of the water than other commercial growers, who, through the application of fertilizer in liquid form, have the possibility of selecting a neutralizing fertilizer, either alkaline or acid in nature. Biodynamic potting soil, made of composts and with a pH of 6.5, will retain its qualities only with a neutral or near neutral water.

It is advisable to remove an excessive iron content, not so much for the sake of plant growth as for the longevity of the watering and plumbing system.

Rare sources for greenhouse water are ponds, rivers or other inland water reservoirs. In each such case, regular sampling is necessary to determine and, if necessary, to avoid undesirable pollutants.

Next to the hydrogen ion concentration, the biodynamic greenhouse grower should put great emphasis on water temperature, a basic factor which is often neglected. Simply stated, the control of water temperature is a must. Each greenhouse crop ideally demands a specific air temperature fluctuation between day and night, with each extreme well-determined. The water temperature for watering the crops has to be related to the air temperature, and specifically to the optimum of the day temperature, because the watering takes place during the day. After many years of observation, I consider the water temperature correct if it exceeds the optimum air temperature by 10°Fahrenheit. With some crops, e.g., cucumber, tomato, basil, 20°F. in excess of air temperature is beneficial.

Once explained, the reason for this practice is easily understood. Like all plant growth, the growth of plants in the greenhouse is forced by temperature, always recognizing, of course, the need for water. The purpose of a greenhouse is to propagate and grow plants when outside temperatures are too low for the specific crop. Heat is the key element in the production of greenhouse crops. The heat in the greenhouse is distributed in measurable degrees in the two basic areas of air and soil. Air temperature will always be higher than soil temperature for both potted plants and benched plants, and even more so for ground growth. The filtered sunlight, entering the greenhouse, is not able to heat the soil as much as it occasionally heats soils in the open. The greater growth stimulant unfortunately comes from a soil warmer than air. This insight leads to heating cables, heating mats, even heated benches or heated pipes in the soil. If we now water our greenhouse plants with cold water, we actually defeat the whole purpose of the greenhouse environment. Watering should strengthen and support what would otherwise be the mere heating of greenhouse air. Warm water raises the soil temperature and thereby promotes plant growth. Additional benefits are better nutrient release, avoidance of shock, and a more resistant plant.

The practice of watering itself, of applying the carrier of life to the greenhouse crops, is probably the major skill of greenhouse management, if we forget for a moment sanitation, soil preparation and fertilization. I have seen greenhouse workers who seemed better able to drench themselves than the thirsty soil. During a lifetime of greenhouse training and management, I can remember with a smile both extremes of water handling. The Sunday water crews in particular are usually in a hurry and mistakenly assume that plants don't need water on Sunday. A Sunday waterer most often flies through the greenhouse like a water fairy, pointing the hose here and there, judging the job done when the skin of the soil has changed its color to a darker shade. The roots go empty and the plants pray for Monday.

Another fellow probably got scolded once for such negligence and decided to apply the water generously, until the boss came running and shouted at him to shut it off. The waters in this case had joined forces and left the greenhouse through the door, because they too had seen enough of the fool who did not even consider flood control. It did not bother the tomatoes, because they can take drenching for a day or two, but it really upset the manager.

Let us get back to the proper practice of watering greenhouse crops. The water can be applied with a watering can, through a rubber hose (don't even consider a plastic hose for the greenhouse), or by a variety of automatic watering systems. The size of a greenhouse operation will determine which option to choose. Watering by hand with a hose is the most practiced method and quite suitable for the biodynamic grower, particularly if crops are grown on benches. Should the biodynamic effort succeed to the extent that vegetables are raised in greenhouses, furrow irrigation would become a further means of watering, especially for a crop like tomatoes.

The element of time is an important factor in watering greenhouse crops. What days or hours are best for watering? Is a Friday better than a Tuesday, or are even hours preferable to the uneven ones? If these questions appeared on an exam, the puzzled student might well wonder what course discussed these details! Time is such an important element, even though Aristotle neglected it entirely.

A good rule of thumb is to water every sunny day, if only

to increase the humidity in the greenhouse. A sunny day will increase air temperature and consequently raise the evaporation of the soil. I personally have adopted the practice of simply taking the hose in the morning as a matter of routine *if* the day starts out sunny. Thus no time is wasted checking the crops and judging whether or not . . . maybe it will get cloudy later . . it really does not look that dry . . . well, I really should have a coffee break first. Positive action from the beginning will make watering a pleasure. I skip those areas which appear moist enough until the next day; only the foliage needs to get a refreshing shower. The plants appreciate such morning misting and will weather the day in a joyous mood, not least of all because the increased humidity makes it so much easier for them to live. The watering expert should not forget to moisten the path, the area under the benches, and even the greenhouse walls under the benches.

The amount of water supplied is definitely in close relation to actual plant growth. It must be kept in mind at all times, however, that the quantity alone is not decisive, but the amount that actually reaches the plant roots. When potted plants are watered, for example, it makes a difference how close the pots are placed to each other and how much water consequently misses the pots altogether. Square pots leave the least space, round pots very little if placed in rows alternately.

A further deciding factor is the depth of the water rim left in the pot. Depending upon the porosity of the growing medium, the pots will be more or less filled with soil. Water is applied to the level pots only as long as it is absorbed by the soil. It should not overflow. With a water rim of about ¼ inch, a good potting soil should handle the water easily, provided it has not dried out too much. A properly watered potted plant should be uniformly moist fifteen minutes after watering. Until one has acquired correct judgment, it is absolutely necessary to unpot a few plants after each watering to visibly check the degree of water penetration. The bottom half of the soil in particular should be evenly moist, because the roots thrive in the lower part of the pot. After watering, no water should be dripping off the benches; this would indicate excessive water use.

The time of day is of utmost importance in watering the greenhouse, even though a strict statement like "watering should be done in the morning hours" is not necessarily correct. Instead, we should look toward the dawn and the evening hours and say that plant foliage should by all means be dry when the sun sets. In order to comply with this requirement during the winter months we certainly have to water in the morning, but on hot summer days we might decide to water during mid-day because a morning watering might not supply enough water to last the rest of the day and through the night. Since plant growth does not stop at night — in fact, in most plants it accelerates — the soil should provide ample water to the plant roots during night hours. But remember, the leaves need to be dry during the sunless, dark hours, especially for the biodynamic greenhouse grower who is concerned about the health of plants. The avoidance of plant diseases begins right here. I am avoiding the word "control" on purpose, because we do not engage in controlling disease; all biodynamic measures in the greenhouse are aimed at producing healthy plants which remain disease-free. The element of water, and the practice of watering, are key factors deciding success or failure in this area.

Water has been described as the carrier of life in a broad and all-pervading sense. In a more practical sense, water also serves as carrier for many substances, some of which are quite important for greenhouse management. All forms of sprays — including the biodynamic sprays — enter the picture at this point, because in all of them water is used as dilutant and carrier.

For biodynamic greenhouse management, liquid fish fertilizer, liquified seaweed, all types of herbal sprays, the biodynamic preparations* 500, 501, valerian (507), and horsetail (508) sprays are used. Wood ashes, dissolved in water, also prove to be a valuable spray. In the greenhouse the application of these growing aids is sensible, almost necessary for proper plant growth and, compared to outside growing, it is easy to carry out. The simplest method is that of siphoning, in which the desired liquid is suctioned out of a container and automatically mixed with the water used for watering the plants. Hardly any extra time is needed to thus apply the desired material to the entire greenhouse growth. Other methods involve the use of watering cans or some form of sprayer. I probably do not need to mention again that the application of all these substances with water, should be done at a time of day which allows the plant to dry off before nightfall.

No discussion of water from a biodynamic point of view would be complete without touching upon the great universal role which water plays, a role which definitely in-

---

*These can be obtained from the Bio-Dynamic Association.

cludes its function in the greenhouse. In the history of the universe, water was given the delicate task of mediating the forces of the moon and governing them for the benefit of all life on earth. Wherever the watery element manifests itself, the moon forces are imbedded in it to an extent determined by the phase of the moon. Knowing of these imponderable influences, the biodynamic greenhouse grower will consciously take steps to regulate water management in such a way that the water will be able to carry the moon forces to those places where they will be of most benefit. In practical terms, this means that seeding, propagation, transplanting, pruning, etc., should be considered, whenever possible, with regard to the moon phase. Such thoughts and considerations establish an awareness of cosmic changes which might, in time, forge a link between plant life and universal life, with the grower as an active participant.

By calling water the carrier of life, our ultimate inquiry might lead to the question of what life is, after all, and where it originates. The conclusion seems to indicate that although water might carry life to the earth, and about and around the earth, the heavenly bodies outside the earth generate life itself. In the final analysis, light, cosmic light, prevails as the eternal source of all forms of life on the planet earth.

CHAPTER 6

Air

After having discussed earth and water, it seems only natural to consider the air element within the greenhouse environment next. How does it resemble the outside climate, and how far has it been removed from the forces of nature itself? There is no doubt in our mind that the element in nature can be devastating to the efforts of gardener or farmer; the greenhouse in this respect might be looked upon as a shelter for plants, or even for the grower himself. This is quite true, but what qualities does the greenhouse-grown plant develop as compared to a tomato which is struggling to reach maturity outside? Little comparative research has been done to my knowledge, and yet it is known of apples that they gain in taste and other qualities if exposed to extreme climate conditions. A "proper upbringing" of our food plants is not to be neglected, for they must also be seen as the source for our spiritual development. The grower ideally should become aware of and accept this responsibility towards others and decide upon growing methods which assure nourishing food for both body and soul. In the greenhouse the grower holds greater responsibility because he supplies and regulates all the requirements for plant growth. In a way, he becomes a substitute for nature forces, for the gods in nature. This aspect of management really cannot be over-emphasized, even when it relates to greenhouse air.

The air in a greenhouse is controlled and regulated by circulation, ventilation, and heating. By definition these three terms are independent of each other, but when applied to a greenhouse environment they are inter-related. Like any other structure, a greenhouse is not, nor should it be, airtight. Even with closed vents and doors, there takes place a constant exchange between inside and outside air. In other words, the air really does not stand still, it constantly moves, it circulates. The degree of circulation depends on the structure of the greenhouse and how tightly glazing or covering materials seal off the air exchange. Do we desire a tight greenhouse? The answer, of course, is that the greenhouse should be as leak-proof as we can possibly get it, the main reason being that the heat-loss during the cold season would be the greater the more air exchange takes place. Another consideration is the possible decision to fumigate the greenhouse interior if such a measure should become necessary. You certainly cannot successfully fumigate a greenhouse which smokes out of all cracks. In general, it might be stated that an air-tight greenhouse is desirable simply because the grower would like to be in control, as much as this is possible.

The uncontrolled circulation, the air movement which takes place in a closed greenhouse, becomes more active if, for example, we open a door. A further and widely adopted practice is to employ electric fans which are built into the greenhouse structure in order to increase air circulation, including most often air exchange. The measurable air flow in the greenhouse can thus be controlled to benefit specific crops or conditions. The most noticeable result is probably the drying effect which fast moving air has upon soil or plant growth.

This discussion of controlled air movement in a greenhouse leads us right into the subject of ventilation. Air vents are installed in greenhouses at the top, the sides, or the ends. All greenhouses — except Quonset-type plastic structures — have top ventilation, again either continuous or partial. At this point it actually becomes necessary to distinguish between the commercial greenhouse grower and the hobby or home grower. Even though the same principles hold true for both, it is the commercial grower who will specialize and select a specific ventilation system chosen entirely to benefit the crop to be grown in the greenhouse.

To be quite clear, thoughts and experiences relate to work with and in mostly glass greenhouses, or those which resemble them in design and ventilation systems. I am aware of the cost factor which, for the commercial grower, often seems to favor a plastic greenhouse: for myself, however, I never could establish a viable, sensible, spiritually rewarding relationship to short-lived, mostly ugly plastic structures. The striving for biodynamic quality somehow does not run parallel with the use of plastic materials. I always like to refer to Goethe, who pointed out that if something is worth doing, it is worth doing well. Could he have included greenhouse building and management? He certainly was a devoted gardening friend and botanist.

The subject still is ventilation, as it relates to green-houses. An all-purpose greenhouse, with benches inside, generally has top ventilation, and side ventilation above the benches. The top at least should have continuous ventilation, meaning that both sides can be opened from end to end. The maximum angle should reach 120 degrees measured from the vertical center of the greenhouse, so that if both top vents are open, the created angle on top will also be 120 degrees. The wide opening allows a large amount of air to move out of the greenhouse quickly, which is especially advantageous in summer. Experience will definitely teach the grower to close the vent to less than 90 degrees during rainy periods because otherwise the water falls right onto the bench.

Without going any further into specific greenhouse designs, the beginning grower may be advised to plan rather for more ventilation capacity than for too little. The subject will briefly be addressed again in the discussion on greenhouse crops.

Even though there are so-called cold greenhouses and what generally is called a pit greenhouse, most greenhouses are designed and built with a heating system. My own experience is limited to coke-fired furnaces, oil-fired hot-forced-air heating systems, and oil-fired hot water furnaces. Coke-fired, or coal-fired greenhouse furnaces are rare nowadays. I came across the last one in 1960 in Pennsylvania. Most older greenhouse units now probably use hot water oil-fired furnaces, while in recent years more and more growers have decided on hot-forced-air with huge fans, often combined with clear plastic tubes distributing the air throughout the greenhouse. The reason for this development again is lower cost. The time factor is rarely included. The motive, in fact, is profit. We in biodynamic work always seem old-fashioned. Why are we concerned about the decline of soil fertility, even aiming to increase fertility, while a faster buck is made by selling turf?

When I see the new contraptions called greenhouses, I really get depressed and pity the plants which have been so far removed from their natural habitat. They seem prisoners of human schemes and technical enslavement. Has anyone looked lately at tomatoes grown commercially in greenhouses? Long plastic bags rest on top of the ground, are filled with a growing-mix, not soil, are constantly supplied with a fertilizer solution, possibly systemic insecticide, and are the home of tomato plants which look like they have been hanged. We never buy tomatoes. We eat our own fresh, when they are in season, and as sauce made from those we put up in jars.

After nearly forty years of greenhouse experience, I, of course, have found my preferred heating system for a greenhouse: oil-fired hot water, with circulator(s). It creates the most constant and most evenly distributed heat in a greenhouse environment. This statement is not meant to discredit or dismiss other heating arrangements; it is really nothing more than subjective preference. In writing about a subject, I like to limit myself to conclusions and results which are based on personal experience alone. I generally do not do what scientists call "research" on the subject, combining and re-phrasing acquired knowledge. In this case, I express myself simply as a grower.

In the old coke-fired heating system the boiler, situated on a lower level than the greenhouses, would heat the water which by physical law would rise and circulate through steel pipes and return to the boiler cooled down.

The greenhouses themselves did not have thermostats, but the temperature had to be regulated by opening or closing pipe valves. The fire in the boiler was controlled by the air intake. Both these regulating skills brought about the desired temperature or temperatures in the greenhouse(s). It was a skill that needed to be learned by experience. Panic broke out when the person in charge would discover at 4 a.m. that the fire in the boiler had died and the greenhouse temperature approached the freezing point.

How easy it is today. All self-controlled by thermostats! The water pipes have fins nowadays to radiate more heat, allowing the use of much thinner pipes which in turn hold less water, thus saving on energy to heat the water. Since in most cases the boiler unit is on the same level as the greenhouse, a circulator forces the water through the pipes. It is still a good idea, and general practice, to locate the water pipes below the benches in the greenhouse. Thereby the plants in the benches receive bottom heat. The warmed air creates its own circulation within the greenhouse, without needing fans to speed the air flow. It is this slow air movement which I particularly like in comparison to hot-forced-air systems. The curious grower can spray water on the hot water pipes and observe how the steam distributes throughout the air without one feeling a draft.

Greenhouses are fascinating environments, and the available choice of ventilation and heating systems offer all degrees of sophistication, allowing for innumerable variations and personal preferences. Whatever the choice, remember, the aim should be a biodynamic home for plants, and not least of all a pleasant working environment for the grower.

Air in the greenhouse not only moves, it also carries. It absorbs warmth, for sure, but it carries water, measured as humidity. Humidity happens to be an important factor in plant growth and health, and therefore needs to be controlled by the grower. The handling of ventilation and heating are part of this control, though the more crucial element is the handling of water itself. The reader may be referred to the section on water.

CHAPTER 7

Light

I said it before: Light is the element of life! Scrub the panes, wash the fiberglass or replace the yellowed polyethelene until the light penetrates the greenhouse covering for the benefit of the plant life. [Refer to the second part of this treatise which deals with sanitation.] Light finds an obstacle in dirt, dust, or algae, all of which will collect on the inside and outside of a greenhouse. The outside is, however, quite often cleaned by rain or snow, while the particles accumulated on the inside urge and invite the greenhouse manager to do something about it. Tools like sponge or brush, in combination with water and soap, offer their services. Extended negligence in this vital area of greenhouse care can easily be noticed by the most inexperienced visitors. Plants in the greenhouse will not cry out for help, they will simply catch an illness much more easily.

It is a definite disadvantage that light has to enter the greenhouse through a man-made material. Part of the light spectrum is reflected and another part is filtered. Greenhouse materials are actually offered with given rates of penetration in reference to the ultraviolet spectrum of the light. Some people select a material by the light penetration factor or whatever it might be called. I personally do not place too much emphasis on this factor and give it at best a second place in considering a choice. My primary concerns are appearance, longevity and low maintenance.

Another reason why a biodynamic grower would not be too intrigued by percentages of light transmission and light penetration is the realization that the light we are concerned about is the sunlight, a cosmic form of energy which makes all plant life possible by supplying both light and warmth. A vast cosmic energy source sends to the planet earth not only a specific form of tremendous radiation, but above all an influx of spiritual forces which nourish the spirituality of all forms of life. A pane of glass or a sheet of polyethelene cannot prevent these forces from reaching the earthly substance. Their blessing does not know such barriers. The grower's awareness of such imponderables and his acknowledgement of spirituality in and around him count more than the greenhouse covering material.

There are other forms of light than sunlight, as we all know. Electric light is often employed in greenhouses to extend what might be called the length of day; or light is used to work in the greenhouse after dark. Whatever the need for additional light, one should realize that electricity originates from the world of sub-nature and is the opposite form of energy from sunlight. I use it sparingly and avoid fluorescent light altogether. In farms and gardens we seldom or will never use artificial light for growing purposes, and right we are, if only because of possible mathematical calculations, including those of the pocketbook. But this aspect leads us naturally to a consideration of the elemental beings within the greenhouse environment.

CHAPTER 8

The Elemental World

With the above question, we leave organic gardening behind and enter the world of biodynamics. The lectures on agriculture by Rudolf Steiner state quite clearly: plant growth is impossible without elemental beings, nature beings, or whatever name someone might prefer. This means the elemental world, or life body, of the earth organism. Will these elemental forces also be active in a greenhouse? It is not a hypothetical question, but rather one which hopefully will awaken a certain degree of awareness in the greenhouse grower who subscribes to the ideas and practices of biodynamic gardening. The question might not sound so unusual if it is re-phrased in a somewhat different way: What in fact would keep elemental forces out of a greenhouse? Certainly not a sheet of plastic or a pane of glass. The greenhouse world is in the same sense penetrated by the elemental world as is the outside world of nature. There is, however, a difference in the degree of care necessary to bring about a normal habitat. The greenhouse world of elemental beings needs more conscious care to fashion the greenhouse into a real home.

The life in the greenhouse is here the guide. We observe and encourage all forms of life which live in harmony with our cultivated crops. Beetles and bees, spiders and wasps, earthworms and occasional bird visitors, like hummingbirds, can all be welcomed and given micro-environments where they belong, and where they reveal by their presence the working of nature forces. The proper managing skill has certainly to be acquired and aligned with control of those insects which are less desirable, but once achieved, it will give the grower unexpected rewards.

The secret — if there really is one — is the constant effort to maintain utmost control, through proper care, of all parts of the greenhouse environment. Again, sanitation is a great part of this control. Do not allow unused spaces to develop into a wasteland or become a dumping ground, but instead create mini-gardens under the benches, for example, for a specific plant species which thrives under the given conditions. Loosen the soil under the benches, rake it, water it, and never allow it to become a dust bin! In time earthworms will help to clean up decaying leaves, toads will check for snails, and bees take charge of pollination. Many of these creatures work at night, avoiding our attention entirely. On one occasion I could not figure out for a long time what power had moved 3-inch pots during the night. Then, one winter evening, late at night when checking temperature, I looked the creature in the eyes: a toad. This was unexpected, I was quite shocked. The fact is, this toad must have jumped each night, for quite some time, four feet high to get into the bench. I am still wondering about this as I write.

As the grower observes, matures, and listens, the presence of elemental beings becomes more of a reality. A greenhouse, in quiet moments, becomes to the observant, unprejudiced person, an entrance to those realms where growth is mediated, possibly much more so than the open field.

CHAPTER 9

Biodynamic Preparations

The biodynamic preparations find full use in greenhouse management. This holds true for the greenhouse ground if used for crop production, for the soil on benches, and for the potting soil used if potted plants are offered for sale. Each one of these diverse operations needs biodynamic compost, though applied and used in different ways. Potting soil and soil for benches has been discussed in an earlier chapter. Ground crops are treated with compost like outdoor crops; i.e., the compost is mixed with the upper five to six inches of the soil. The degree of decomposition of the compost material itself should be complete for all applications; for potting soil an earthlike, fine appearance is necessary. This means that the compost for potting soil will possibly be three years old in our northern climate. The biodynamic preparations: yarrow (502), camomile (503), nettle (504), oak bark (505), dandelion (506) and valerian (507) should be inserted into the compost pile during the first year of maturing. There is no harm done if the compost pile is treated again the second year.

The use and application of horn manure (Preparation 500) will probably be approached in different ways by the individual grower, depending upon his understanding and experience and the time frame of the entire operation. It will often be hard to justify stirring a portion for one hour if only a pint is needed. It would seem reasonable to treat the greenhouse in this respect as an extension of the outside activity, if there are gardens or fields to be worked. I personally find it easier to treat the compost pile in the second year with the Biodynamic Compost Starter,* which includes the horn manure in addition to the other preparations. Thereby the benefit of the horn manure becomes available for all greenhouse soil requirements.

Horn silica (Preparation 501) is a more difficult issue, especially if the greenhouse harbors plants in all stages of growth, from seedlings to mature specimens. The simplest condition exists if there is only one crop in the greenhouse, all tomatoes, or all lettuce, for example. In such a case the handling of horn silica is the same as outside use. My biodynamic greenhouse experience is limited to herb growing, and after an initial use of horn silica I decided not to use it either for broad or partial application.

A logical explanation for my reasons is hard to formulate. An intuitive understanding of the working of horn silica seems to bring a realization that the effects of the horn silica are not entirely limited to the plant surfaces

---

*Available from the Pfeiffer Foundation, 241 Hungry Hollow Rd., Spring Valley, N.Y. 10977

which are sprayed, but radiate beyond the sprayed area. The effect is not a mutual interaction between donor and recipient only, as is the case with horn manure. The horn silica seems to enter at a point but then expands in its workings into a larger sphere. The resulting effect, especially on young seedlings and cuttings, is of a more retarding nature than desirable. A reasonable explanation is the fact that here the root pole needs stimulation and vitalization; horn silica, however, relates to the opposite, to the ripening pole. At any rate, I like to caution the prospective greenhouse grower and encourage his detailed observation to see if horn silica application should be considered in greenhouses with plants in various stages of growth.

CHAPTER 10

Fertilization

The subject of plant nutrition in a biodynamically managed greenhouse is less of a primary concern than in other commercial greenhouse operations. Compost is the basic fertilizing substance used, both for ground cultivation and bench growing. The required soil for potted plants is furnished by blending various composts and the other ingredients discussed in Chapter 4. The use of so-called organic fertilizers needs possible clarification. All solid organic fertilizers, like bone meal, cotton seed meal, blood meal, rock phosphate, etc. are best added to the composting process from the very beginning. Again, the major concern here is that no decay or breakdown should actually occur inside the greenhouse, with the exception of specialty crops (cucumber, for example) which require a different manure/compost handling.

Another group are the liquid organic fertilizers: fish emulsion, liquid seaweed concentrate, liquid nettle manure, liquid fermented chicken manure, and the like. These fellows offer their service and benefits at a price: their pungent, peculiar, sometimes even obnoxious odors come along with them. If the grower finally seems to get used to it all, it often turns out that the family members, or even the greenhouse visitors, will not. It is a real dilemma, because what else in the organic fertilizer realm can push plant growth better than this stinking, rotten, liquid, fermented chicken manure! Nettle is not quite as bad — but seaweed is really the most pleasant liquid fertilizer.

I would like to evaluate them first in summary. Seen through biodynamic spectacles, nearly all of them — the exception possibly being nettle — fail to qualify for graduation. They are crutches used as an emergency measure to save some inadequately conceived and implemented biodynamic greenhouse fertilizer program. A soil supplied with proper, high-quality biodynamic composts does not need these "fragrant fellows." The money which would be required to buy them should rather be spent on good old cow manure. This is the organic substance which, with biodynamic composting methods, will turn into stable humus, pleasing the plant roots for months on end.

Liquid seaweed can be built into a spray program aiming at achieving and maintaining plant growth healthy enough to shrug off diseases and undesirable insects. (See Chapters 14 and 15.)

Fish emulsion has always been well advertised, much more so than biodynamic compost, and it has a certain place in organic horticulture/agriculture. An inexperienced greenhouse grower should by all means gather his or her own experience of it with those crops that grow close to their hearts. I would judge it least suitable for potted plants which are exposed to nearly daily watering over a long period of time. The fish emulsion seems to proliferate the formation of algae on the surface of the soil in pots, thereby sealing off the normal water penetration. A misting-on, or foliar feeding alone, is probably the best application of fish emulsion in greenhouses.

Liquid fermented chicken manure is an old-fashioned fertilizing agent for both indoor and outdoor fertilization of mature plants during their peak growing stage. Being high in all basic nutrients (N = 1.65%, P_2O_5 = 1.55%, K = 0.85%, Ca = 2.42%) this liquid always gets results. Of course, it can by no means be called a biodynamic booster shot, simply because this growth aid was invented before biodynamic methods were offered. Nevertheless, it is an acceptable organic measure to support otherwise weak, under-nourished vegetation. Furthermore, no one prevents the biodynamic grower from hanging bags with the biodynamic preparations into the liquid during the fermentation process.

In practical terms the preparation of the liquid is as follows: Take about 10 pounds of pure chicken manure (from under the roost), add it to about 25 gallons of water and stir; stir a few times a day until the fermentation slows down. Whatever floated on top at first should have sunk to the bottom. The length of time depends on temperature, but expect three weeks at any rate. The resulting liquid is now the concentrate for fertilizing purposes.

Application is generally done with a watering can; if the spout of the can is rather fine, a straining of the liquid through cheesecloth might be necessary. A three-gallon watering can could take about a pint of the fermented chicken manure liquid. Exact proportions are not that critical; if in the beginning more chicken manure is added to a given volume of water, then less of the resulting concentrate needs to be taken for watering. For frequency of application it is better to apply smaller amounts more often than larger amounts of the liquid only once. The grower should be aware that the liquid is alkaline and therefore not suitable for acid-soil loving plants.

Old and proven is the practice of making a liquid herb manure from the cut nettle plants. The available amount is submerged in water and allowed to decompose in it. Over a period of three weeks, the liquid will undergo a kind of fermentation which completely digests the nettle plants, leaving a few fibers only. During and especially after this period the nettle liquid is a valuable aid in plant growth and protection. Diluted or undiluted it can be sprayed on any plant with the result, that the treated plants will respond with vigorous and healthy growth. In my own work with plants, I have often encouraged many crops to continue growing with this liquid, despite sometimes adverse conditions.

Wood ashes are also a source of fertilization for greenhouse crops. Many of us use wood furnaces again, or have a fireplace where ashes accumulate. The yearly supply of ash might not be sufficient for an outside garden but could possibly fulfill the greenhouse requirement. Unleached wood ashes have between 5% and 6% potash, 2% of phosphoric acid, and 30% of lime. Care should be taken when storing the wood ashes. Leaching, saturation with water during storage, can wash out nearly all potash, which is the most desirable element in wood ashes.

For greenhouse use, the wood ashes are also added to water, although they do not require a fermentation phase. A generous amount of wood ash is dumped into a bucket of water and the mixture stirred. The charcoal particles will float, and the mineral part will settle to the bottom. The resulting liquid is a highly alkaline substance and, if a great amount of ash has been used, will actually be a lye and burn the skin, dissolving the upper cells. Therefore use only a wooden stick for stirring and do not get any liquid into your eyes. The charcoal is screened off and the liquid best strained and kept for immediate and/or future use. The liquid is again treated as a concentrate, using about a cupful for two gallons of water. Watering with this diluted wood-ash fertilizer serves two purposes: it maintains the desired pH of frequently watered soil, and it supplies a fair amount of potash and phosphate especially to flowering and seed-bearing plants. Naturally, it would be counterproductive for acid-loving plants.

CHAPTER 11

Spray Schedule

Biodynamic greenhouse growers at one time or another will certainly be asked what they do against diseases and insects, which are somehow always considered unavoidable. Insects, meaning destructive insects, of course — beneficial ones are usually not considered at all. An extension of the question generally is: what do you spray to "control" — the accurate term being "kill" — them? I have often used such an opening question to begin "lecturing," provided the time was there and the mood was right.

There are two major ways of responding. Is the average person able to think of spraying only as an effort to work *against* something, and is a solution expected only if some form of life is killed, in order to "protect" another form? Plant protection is the scientific term. This little chapter is meant to explain that spraying can also be done *for* something — for the support of life, for strengthening of growth forces, for guidance of insect life.

Proper biodynamic greenhouse management should set

up from the very beginning a routine spraying program, implemented during the main growing season(s) and scrupulously executed in a rhythmical manner. The choice of materials is up to the grower and the demand of the crop(s). The basic sprays, in my opinion, should be horsetail tea (508), the biodynamic valerian preparation (507), camomile tea, and liquid seaweed. I would also consider woodashes and nettle manure (see previous chapter).

Each week one material is simply prepared and sprayed in the morning prior to watering. Watering itself should be held back until the plants have dried or else eliminated altogether on that particular day. Only a misting is needed; the spray material should not necessarily drop off the leaves. It is not the volume that assures success; it is the effort and the spray material that counts. There really seems no need to describe how to prepare the various spray materials. Biodynamic literature is full of these details.* But do not neglect to boil the horsetail (*Equisetum arvense*) for fifteen minutes. The resulting fragrance is a free reward for the human soul in the process.

The idea behind such a spraying schedule is quite simple. The plants are offered forces inherent in the spray materials which help overcome the deficiency of sun forces encountered in a greenhouse environment. This practice, in conjunction with proper temperature control, will result in plant growth which is firm, not lush, resistant, not inviting. Remember, light is the element of life!

---

*See "*Bio-Dynamic Sprays,*" H.H. Koepf (Bio-Dynamic Association 1971)

CHAPTER 12

Greenhouse Crops

There may be many reasons why a person decides to become a greenhouse grower, and yet two categories may be clearly distinguished: the commercial grower and the hobby greenhouse gardener. The latter will have more leisure and less pressure — unless it comes from a marriage partner — while the first has greater challenges and more satisfaction from a successful operation.

Most greenhouses certainly provide a home for a variety of plants, especially those which are offered in flats or pots. Benches are the rule in these houses, so handling of and caring for the plants on the benches is rather simple and physically easy. Everyone knows this type of greenhouse; all florists have a number of them.

The home grower would have the same type, of manageable size. Suitable crops include all annual and perennial flowers, succulents, cacti, ferns, herbs, dwarf evergreens, orchids, etc. For vegetable growing, the benches are filled

71

with at least 8 inches of soil and the plants either seeded directly into the soil or transplanted from flats or pots. (See again chapter 4.) Easiest to grow are radishes, all lettuce varieties, parsley, cress, short carrots, kohlrabi; requiring a little more green thumb are cucumbers, cauliflower, peppers, tomatoes.

The commercial grower is easily tempted by market conditions and demand to grow specific crops in the greenhouse on a large scale for the local market. Here comes the challenge. The primary crop in demand all year round will be tomatoes.* Properly managed, they behave predictably in greenhouses and bring a fair price per square foot of greenhouse space. Two requirements have to be kept in mind: 1) tomatoes are heavy feeders and have to be supplied with optimum nutrition (meaning compost) and water to achieve a yield which more than covers total expenses, including labor and greenhouse depreciation; 2) tomatoes need air movement for pollination and disease-free growth. Stagnant, moist, warm air is detrimental to permanent tomato culture. This last requirement led to the designing of a specific tomato greenhouse which provided optimum air circulation. (See page 73.)

The tomatoes are trained on strings as one-stemmed or two-stemmed; the strings are attached to horizontal wires which are held by posts at each end of the greenhouse. Once the plants begin to flower, these wires are shaken with their hanging plants so that the pollen separates from the blossom and travels with the air. In order to be effec-

---

*For more information, see BIODYNAMICS #51, The Tomato, H. Grotzke

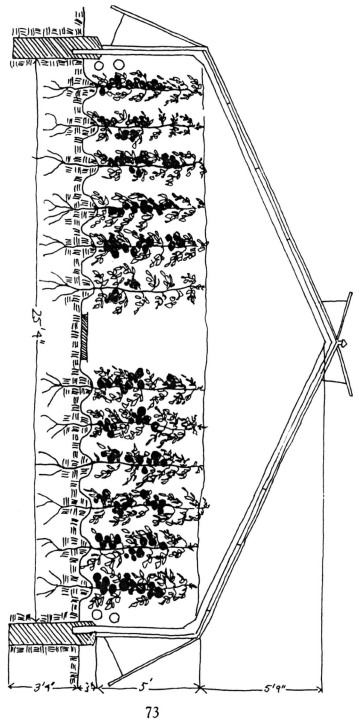

Specially designed tomato greenhouse

25'4"

3'4" 3' 5' 5'9"

tive, the plant must be dry; early afternoon is a good time.

Watering the tomatoes is done in such a way that the water does not actually touch the leaves but irrigates the soil alone. Drip irrigation nowadays seems a favorite method. Water temperature should not be lower than soil temperature.

As mentioned earlier, more "modern" greenhouses — also those for tomatoes — are probably of the plastic Quonset type. All criteria, however, remain the same. Air movement will have to be brought about by mechanical/electrical means. All other practices apply equally well. The tomatoes should be harvested only when red in order to achieve the best quality and taste and to triumph over the out-of-state competition.

Another intriguing and challenging greenhouse crop is the cucumber. Cucumbers prefer growing conditions nearly opposite to those for tomatoes: warm temperature, high humidity, no air movement. The ideal greenhouse is structured accordingly (see page 75). The center is no higher than 8 feet and the width about 12 feet with a walk in the middle.

The cucumbers are planted in hills with a distance of four feet between and tied to wires as they grow.* Important points to remember are: 1) cucumbers are heavy feeders and thrive best in a highly organic medium; 2) watering is best done as misting, with warm water only; 3) cucumbers are shallow rooters and might need a top dressing of compost if roots begin to show on the surface; 4) you

---

*For more information, see BIODYNAMICS #64, The Cucumber, H. Grotzke.

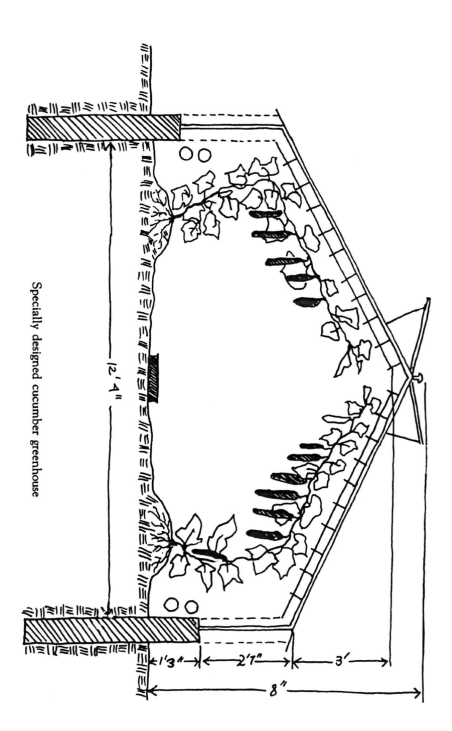

Specially designed cucumber greenhouse

12' 4"

1'3"   2'7"   3'

8"

should avoid walking on the soil — use permanent boards to walk on; 5) if time permits, you can pinch off the male flowers to avoid seed formation in the cucumbers; 6) you must keep as uniform a temperature for night and day as possible. After all these minor considerations are taken care of, the grower will have the major satisfaction of watching the cucumbers grow and harvesting them when they reach the desirable size.

Possibly the easiest greenhouse vegetable crops are all varieties of lettuce. Lettuce is more modest in nutrient and heat requirements than any of the above. In order to establish a crop, transplants are preferred to direct seeding. Otherwise cultivation is not much different from outdoor growing. Timing is somewhat crucial for an economic operation, because the short mid-winter days will not produce much growth. Temperature fluctuation between day and night is healthy for lettuce; fuel expense is therefore lower than for tomatoes and cucumbers. Since the crop is short-lived, it is possible, with proper timing, to interplant lettuce with tomatoes.

The cabbage crops are inviting to experiment with. The easiest is kohlrabi, followed by kale, then broccoli and finally cauliflower. Our own freezer-dominated life-style unfortunately makes it unnecessary to grow these crops in the greenhouse. I grow them outside in the summer for eating during the growing season and freeze the rest for winter use.

CHAPTER 13
─────────────────

Cuttings

Most greenhouses for general use set aside a fair amount of space for plant propagation. Sale of seedlings and plants in trays are a reliable source of income in the spring.

Plants can be propagated in various ways. The most common and generally easiest procedure is to sow seeds of the desired plant species. Other means of propagation are division, layering, grafting, budding and, of course, the method of rooting stem cuttings. Each plant species is propagated one way or the other, though some plants can be reproduced from seed only, while others merely from cuttings, or by one of the other above-mentioned methods. Propagation from cuttings requires the most controlled conditions and skill and is therefore best performed in a greenhouse.

In order to successfully root cuttings, some fundamental experience and knowhow are needed. So this phase of plant propagation shall be discussed in more detail here, in order to encourage the home-gardener and perhaps even give some new ideas to the professional grower. The emphasis will be on herbs, since many of them must be reproduced by cuttings.

Among the plants which are generally grown from cuttings are the various kinds of geraniums and begonias, then such herbs as tarragon, southernwood, rosemary, santolina, and many others. The technique and the practical steps in rooting a cutting are similar with each plant species except the time element, which in the matter of when to do it, needs individual attention. The cutting of one plant might, for example, root better in spring than in fall or vice versa.

The practical process of propagation by cuttings can be divided into five distinct steps, each of which requires careful preparation and performance. They are:

1. Choosing the rooting medium,
2. Preparing the cutting,
3. Making the cut,
4. Planting the cutting,
5. Caring for the cutting.

Over the years, various rooting media have been used and tested. It actually is a personal choice of the grower; results have been achieved with pure sand as well as pure peat. Lately even substances of mineral or chemical nature have been used to root cuttings. My own rooting mixture has evolved from practical experience and comparison, combined with the biodynamic approach to nature. What is expected from the rooting medium? To guarantee a uniform formation of roots within a reasonable time! The cutting can here be compared with the seed, because both root formation and seed germination require the presence of the three elements — air, warmth, and water. Therefore the rooting medium must be of such a nature as to play host to these three elements, the ratio of which are decisive as well. The rooting medium must care for the equilibrium between air, warmth, and water. If one dominates, the root formation can be disturbed or even prevented. Water, for example, in excessive amounts, may cause the cutting to mold or rot; while too much air dries out the wound of the cut. So the right rooting mixture is obviously important.

Many a grower has probably used sand — river-sand to be exact — all his life and successfully propagated plants. Sand has the advantage of correcting mistakes of overwatering, and always allows enough air to reach the stem end in the ground, even if it is planted too deep. Thus the porous structure of sand is intensively made use of. A word of caution may be repeated here: Wash every sand before using it, also river-sand! It is possible that sand (whatever the source) may contain toxic water-soluble salts which would interfere with a normal root formation. Also organic impurities are washed out at the same time. For this purpose the sand is dumped into a container, clean water added and the sand stirred. After it has settled again, the cloudy water is drained off and this procedure repeated until the water stays clean.

In my opinion, pure sand also has a disadvantage: It stimulates the cutting to produce roots which are not earthly; meaning, they are different from those which grow in common soil. To clarify and illustrate this statement, let us consider some soil principles.

For our purpose it is sufficient to divide the soil into the following components: Silica (sand), clay, calcium, and organic matter or humus. The first three are the mineral ingredients, combined and buffered by the organic matter which turns into humus through soil-life activity. The varying amounts of these components determine the type of soil. The clay particles are the smallest, the silicious particles the largest, excepting gravel and stones. Plant roots adjust to the soil type and differ in their appearance and growth. Roots growing in pure sand look different from those growing in an ordinary garden soil. The reason why can be better understood with reference to the agricultural lectures which Dr. Steiner gave in 1924. According to his insight, earthly and cosmic forces meet in the earth and influence plant growth. Silica in the form of sand or quartz, and calcium in the form of limestone deposits and alkaline humus complexes are servants of two opposite streams which collide in the soil and are immediately balanced again by the clay substance. The silica as soil ingredient exists to assimilate the forces reaching down to earth from the distant planets, while the calcium in the soil attracts earthly formative forces, including those from the Moon and the near planets Mercury and Venus. How do such invisible energies become apparent in plants?* They appear in the growth habit of the whole plant and in the physical expression of its distinct parts. The diameter of roots, for example, is the thinner the sandier the soil. Then too, the amount of essential oils in plants diminishes with the decrease of sand in soils. Each plant adjusts to the type of soil from the moment it germinates and

---

*See *"Planetary Influences Upon Plants,"* Kranich (Bio-Dynamic Association 1984)

takes hold of the earth with its roots. The same holds true for cuttings.

The root formation of a cutting in pure sand is completely determined by the cumulative forces which have been absorbed by the sand. The roots are thin and long, and look like the result of severe starvation. They wish to feel and grasp the earth yet find nothing but sand, a medium high in planetary forces only. So the rooted cuttings have soon to be shifted to pots with earthly food in the potting mixture. But now a complete readjustment of each single root has to take place, before the actual food intake can begin. This phenomenon can be compared to a person who has fasted for many days and suddenly is exposed to an abundance of food. Illness can be the result. I decided therefore to avoid such an occurrence by composing a rooting medium which combines all the main and necessary soil ingredients. From the above discussion it became clear that they must be:

$$\begin{array}{rl} \text{Silica} - & \text{Sand (Hybrotite)} \\ \left.\begin{array}{r} \text{Calcium} \\ \text{Clay} \end{array}\right\} & \text{Humus Soil} \\ \text{Organic Matter} - & \text{Spaghnum Moss} \end{array}$$

So the final mixture consists of equal parts of hybrotite, earthworm compost, and moss.

In order to eliminate locating and washing ordinary sand, I prefer to use Hybrotite. This is a proven commercial product of crushed granite stone, and therefore of a pure nature. Hybrotite seems to directly stimulate root formation through its particle size and structure. It will be remembered that sand granules are nearly round and within a narrow range of size. The crushed granite, on the other hand, ranges in size from dust to almost gravel, and the individual particles are irregularly cornered. These characteristics are ideal for thorough penetration of the whole mixture. Where Hybrotite cannot be had, sand must suffice, and, if washed, will also prove satisfactory. It will not always be possible to reach ideal conditions but they ought to be mentioned.

A rich humus soil is added to the mixture not only for calcium and clay, but also for plant nutrients. The chosen compost has to be fully ripe to eliminate any further decomposition. My preference goes to an earthworm compost, which is a completely digested material, rich in nutrients as well as calcium. The pH ranges between 8.0 and 8.5, allowing for the acid moss part. Clay is present, in a humus-rich compost, as part of the clay-humus-complex. This earthworm compost in the rooting mixture offers food to the roots as soon as they are formed, and allows the grower more time for shifting the rooted cuttings to pots. A week or more of delay does not harm the young plants because they steadily keep on growing due to the nutrients found in the mixture.

Spaghnum moss finally is the purely organic substance in this mixture and thus balances out the sand. While the sand barely holds water, the moss absorbs and holds quantities. The time for watering the cuttings is thereby shortened, though it requires a little more observation and feeling. Besides its water storing capacity, the moss is chosen for its ability to check diseases. Moss is a primitive plant which, by its nature and properties, is immune to disease and consequently incorporates such qualities into the rooting medium. Before the moss is mixed with the other ingredients, it should be nearly saturated with water.

Hybrotite, humus-soil, and moss are then mixed. The mixture should be fairly moist but not wet. After it has been decided what place to use for cuttings, the rooting mixture is filled either into the prepared area or into flats. The choice for the rooting bed should include considerations for temperature and light. Good root formation needs warmth in soil and air. A slightly warmer soil temperature has proved beneficial for faster rooting and very often can be had by utilizing space over heating pipes, radiators, etc. Temperature and rooting mode are closely related. Though rooting will take place over a wider range of temperature, it starts within a shorter time at moderately higher temperatures. The minimum soil temperature may be set at 50°F with at least the same air temperature. Much faster root formation will, however, be achieved at a temperature of 70 - 75°F. Therefore many cuttings root much more readily in late summer than in early spring, though factors other than temperature also influence the results.

An equal importance must be given to the light requirements of the cuttings. Full sunlight will not be necessary, but the location should not be in total shade either. The process of assimilation has to continue in the cutting to assure a good formation. It is always easier to shade the rooting bed than to solve, for example, problems of rotting which might be caused by a lack of sunlight.

Finally the mixture is spread over the area or filled into the flats so as to get a workable rooting bed of at least two inches thickness. The advantage of using flats is that they can be moved, allowing for a more flexible and often space-saving operation. The rooting medium is levelled and then lightly packed with a little board or similar tool. The packing is done to assure a good soil density. Now the bed is ready to receive the cuttings.

In general, material used for cuttings is taken from the tips of the plants to be propagated. In the case of large perennials it is advisable to cut from the lower branches since these cuttings respond better in forming roots. The length of the cuttings varies with the different plants but, if possible, they should be about 3 inches long to start with. The procedure can best be explained in two steps. First the material to be rooted is cut, and then the cutting is prepared for planting. Tender plants and annuals can be cut with knife or scissors, while for more woody plants pruning shears are best used. The time for making cuttings depends upon the plant, usually spring or late summer are chosen.

The cutting is prepared for planting by taking the lower leaves off the stem. Provided the sprig is 3 inches long, it may serve as a guide to remove the leaves halfway, leaving a top of 1½ inches. The leaves have to be taken off carefully to avoid damage to the stem. The idea is to have as little wounded surface as possible, because all this area loses moisture. The best practice is to cut the leaves with a sharp knife, and pinch off those of tender annuals with the fingernails. Never strip or tear the tender bark or cut into the stem!

After these preparatory steps, the sprig is ready for the final cut. Making this cut correctly will take you at least a third of the way to success. A sharp knife is a necessity. The cut has to be clean, which is achieved by pulling the knife through the stem — not by pressing it through. All injured tissues of an organism heal faster if the wound is a clean cut. This holds true also for plant tissue, and in rooting it is especially important since the formation of roots will occur only after the open cut has closed. This is brought about by a formation of new cells, called callus, along the cut. The sharper the knife and the better the cut, the faster callus will form. Roots start to grow from the callus and/or the stem, depending upon the plant.

At this point the question of growth substances might be mentioned. Many are on the market and in use, as for example Hormo-Root, Proliferol, Rootone, Transplantone. In my work Rootone is the only one I have used for experiment and comparison. For most of my cuttings though, I had the possibility of trying an extraction of various wild herbs, which compared favorably with Rootone and the cuttings rooted without any treatment. The result from the use of these various growth substances will probably be different with each individual grower. My suggestion would be to first try without them, or at least make equal plantings of treated and untreated cuttings and actually see whether or not a response can be observed. Old-time growers had a different method of stimulating root formation. They split the lower part of the stem and inserted a kernel of oats. This would germinate and at the same time aid the rooting process of the cutting, due to — as was later found — the release of growth hormones from the sprouting oat seed. Most rooting aids on the market today still use hormone preparations, though others have shifted to synthetic chemicals (indolebutyric acid, alphanaphthalene acetic acid) to induce root formation.

Now the cutting is ready for planting. The spacing should be such that each cutting stands free without touching the other, allowing ample air circulation. A planting in marked rows, for a larger amount of cuttings, gives the whole operation a professional look. The sprig is planted by pushing it straight down into the rooting medium, not more than 1 inch deep. It must be realized that proper aeration must be guaranteed and might be lacking in the deeper layers. The stem end must be well surrounded by the soil. Very tender and soft cuttings may not penetrate the soil and break when you try to push them down. In such cases a hole has to be made first with a little stick and the cutting is then planted, making sure the soil is packed around the stem again. Good soil contact is essential.

Within an hour the planted cuttings and with them the rooting medium are moistened with a fine spray of water. The soil should be moist but not wet or over-saturated. From now on the cuttings need daily care until they are rooted, which takes about three weeks. The cuttings themselves serve as a guide. They never should show signs of wilting, which is prevented by watering and shading. The watering, of course, depends upon the humidity of the building or coldframe where the cuttings are kept. In general, they will need a light watering every day except on very warm days when high evaporation calls for additional watering. As a disease preventive measure it is a good rule to water the cuttings in the forenoon only, so the leaves will be dried off by night. On very cloudy and rainy days watering may not be necessary. If in spite of all the care a cutting decides to rot, pull it out and use camomile tea instead of water and check whether the soil has already been over-watered. Allow ample ventilation for the rooting bed.

Shading will be necessary during the first two weeks if the rooting bed is exposed to full sunlight. Various materials can be used, but cheesecloth proved better than any other. It should be well above the cuttings and removed after the sun passes by.

On the average it takes about three weeks until the cuttings root. A check can be made by pulling on one of the upper leaves. The cutting has rooted if the leaf tears off; it pulls out altogether if no or very few roots have formed. The roots should have reached a length of at least 1 inch before the new plant is shifted to pots. Very long roots can be cut off with scissors. The pot size is determined by the root development but should in the beginning be small. The soil used in the pots is a regular potting mixture or a good garden soil.

Having success with cuttings is no art, everyone can learn it. In summarizing, the three decisive steps should be remembered. They are: 1) the correct rooting medium, 2) a clean cut with a sharp knife, and 3) particular daily care of the cuttings.

In conclusion here is a list of a few plants which are easily propagated by cuttings. Try one or two for a start.

PEPPERMINT: One of the easiest to root. Use the tips of the new shoots with leaves developed, preferably in spring. Wilting occurs soon, so moisten the leaves often. Cuttings will root in less than three weeks.

ROSEMARY: A very attractive plant, propagated by cuttings for centuries. The best time to start them is late fall, after the first frost has come. Varieties root differently, the white-blooming one roots best.

GERANIUM: All geraniums can be used for cuttings. January and February is the right time if they are supposed to bloom by May. All branched side leaves should be removed, leaving the center leaves (at least three) only. A clean cut is essential, so is shallow planting.

BEGONIA: Very easy to root. Both wilting and rotting have to be checked, though. Be sure cuttings are dry before night.

SOUTHERNWOOD: Another herb which is propagated by cuttings only. They root readily if taken in late fall, same as rosemary.

THYME: This plant roots very easily at any time of the year. Outdoor cuttings are best since they do not wilt as readily as indoor growth. The leaves tend to rot, so make sure they are dry during nights and cloudy days.

CHAPTER 14
_____

Insects

This chapter is not included to scare the grower, even though most often the reference to insects probably has a negative sound. The biodynamic grower, however, should not be frightened by insects. Insects are a part of nature, like you and me, assuming in this case that human individuals are in fact a part of nature. The insects might entirely disagree, because they keep observing human creatures (with the exception of the biodynamic grower, of course) constantly attacking and destroying nature. There should be an inner harmony and understanding between the insect world and the human soul of the biodynamic grower; there simply must be, after one studies and implements all the available material on the relationship between nature and the human being.

A greenhouse environment is certainly more sensitive to the attunement of the grower and his or her actions; it cannot be any other way, because life in the greenhouse

— especially plant life, of course — is entirely dependent upon the grower. All creatures in the greenhouse hope for a benevolent and initiated individual who will enter into a silent conversation with what Rudolf Steiner called the etheric and astral spheres. There is no doubt that the insects participate in this dialogue, and insects will always be there. The initial establishment of communication is definitely to get to know them. Any plant, whether inside or outside the greenhouse, should always be viewed, in the imagination, with its surrounding insect world, above and below ground, regardless of the effect of this world upon the plant itself. Plant and insect form one picture, for which we might not have a name, and yet their mutual existence is a reality.

Upon entering the greenhouse, the bearer of greenhouse karma should simply leave outside all prejudices and misconceptions related to insects. I have witnessed occasions where the responsible person did more damage to plant growth than any insect would ever have done; remember this possibility upon entering. To enter a greenhouse in full consciousness — provided all distractions are held back — is like stepping into a different world. Temperature is different, light and fragrance are different, the intensity of growth forces is different, even the sound is different. It might take some skill for the grower to discard all the inner accumulation of detailed data in order to make room for perceptions of this kind, but let nobody persuade you it is a vain attempt.

The aim of the biodynamic grower should be to maintain a level of what we are used to calling destructive insects which can be tolerated within the range of acceptable damage to crops. It must be recognized that there is no such thing, not even in chemically controlled environments, as an insect-free space on earth. Therefore we should not even expect to walk around in a greenhouse without insects. To make a long story short, my intention is nothing more than to convince the current or prospective greenhouse manager to leave behind all fear of insects. Once this has been accomplished, an amazing experience will eventually occur if customers or friends are allowed to visit the greenhouse. The question certainly will be, "Do you know you have aphids (white flies, mites, etc.) on your plants?" The unspoken part of the question is whether or not you are doing anything about it.

I should make it quite clear that I by no means promote the greenhouse as an insect-breeding institution! Whoever has read up to this point will have realized that biodynamic greenhouse management is entirely different from, let us call it, orthodox management. Three basic conditions have to be met if one is to expect a certain degree of success: 1) the theoretical and practical understanding of the interrelationships between plant, insect, and the grower; 2) the sanitation of the entire greenhouse environment; and 3) the routine implementation of a preventive spraying program with the substances discussed earlier. If all these criteria are met, little should happen to cause an emergency. Still, emergencies will occasionally develop, if only due to neglect. A greenhouse needs daily care, and the tasks do not take a vacation, as the person-in-charge might feel justified in doing.

Aphids are in general the first to appear. They prefer the tender tips of plants or whatever soft tissue is available. An infestation can occur rather fast because their reproductive cycle is impressive. Constant observation is necessary to judge whether or not the routine spraying program, already in place, will limit or reduce the population. The ash-spray might have to be moved up to attempt a slowdown of infestation. The concentration of the spray could be increased if non-sensitive plants are affected. Silica powder or diatomaceous earth could be dusted. A check the following day will reveal the results. Have aphids dropped off the plants? Are they still alive? How do those look which are clinging to the plants? Take a close look, with a magnifying glass. Many insects have some of the ugliest features displayed in nature. Often these features reveal how the insect causes damage to plants, and by seeing them we can get a better idea of how we might discourage their feedings.

Sometimes prevention does not work; then discouragement also fails. What next? The grower might decide to become less observant and more aggressive. At this juncture there are two alternatives, both utilizing toxic substances: fumigation and spraying. I personally prefer fumigation, which is possible in a tight greenhouse. This consideration is another reason to build a greenhouse well so it can be controlled entirely, even with regard to the use of fumigation. The advantage of fumigation is that no residues are left on the foliage. For the biodynamic grower there is only one fumigation material, nicotine. It comes in tin cans and is ignited in the greenhouse at dusk, when bees have left the greenhouse. Nicotine is harmful to aphids, leafhoppers, mealybugs, lace bugs, spider mites and thrips.

Spraying with various substances chosen for specific insect control is an old practice in greenhouses. Fortunately, with biodynamic methods the need for such direct measures will be much smaller, even negligible, when compared to orthodox commercial greenhouse management. It must be realized that even though the biodynamic grower has an impressive selection of so-called natural insecticides at his disposal, these plant poisons should be used only as a last resort. The drawback is their broad-spectrum effect upon insects; in other words, they are not selective with regard to the species they reduce. Compared to chemical insecticides, however, they are much safer for human beings. The list of these natural plant poisons includes rotenone, pyrethrum, sabadilla dust, ryania, and nicotine sulfate. During the last few years so-called insecticidal soaps have extended the grower's range of choice. Each individual should get to know the substances and select the one that he/she can be most comfortable with. For a number of justifiable reasons, I prefer nicotine sulfate, even though it is the most dangerous one to handle. The advantages are that its nitrogen part acts like a fertilizer and the breakdown in light is fast.

You will need to apply the spray of your choice with some sort of sprayer. In more than thirty years of greenhouse work, one cannot help but try them all: the knapsack sprayer, the pressure sprayer, the trombone sprayer, etc. It is very hard to find a high-quality piece of equipment. For the greenhouse it makes sense to acquire an electric sprayer, an atomizer, because it achieves the best results with the least amount of spray material. Due to the high blast, the spray also reaches the underside of leaves and deposits the material as a fine mist, without dropping excess on the soil. The initial outlay for an atomizer might seem prohibitive, but the saving of time and material over

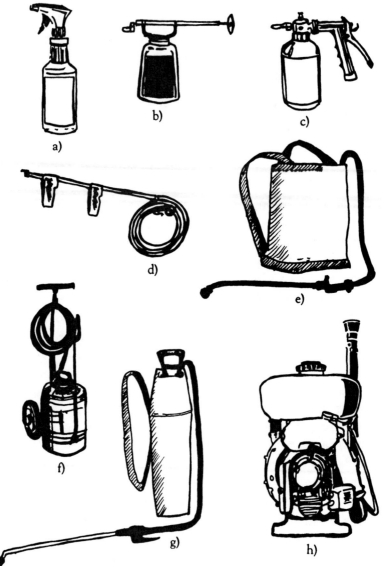

Examples of sprayers: a) trigger, b) gun, c) hose, d) trombone,
e) knapsack, f) cart, g) tank, h) motor mist

a long period of operation justifies the expense.

Biological control of insects is another area in which advances have been made during the last few years. My own experience in this field is rather limited, but I cannot help noticing the offerings made in the specific sales literature. Once I purchased the lady beetle bugs which are known to feed on aphids and were offered at the time to reduce aphid infestations in the greenhouse. In this case there definitely was an abundance of aphids on young vegetable plants, especially cabbages, cauliflowers, peppers, etc. The shipment of lady beetles arrived in good condition, and the beetles were released in the greenhouse according to instructions. It was a glass greenhouse. The lady bug beetles departed in all directions, searching for food, I assumed.

The next morning I once more learned that human logic and the realities of living things are not necessarily the same. Countless lady beetles, with their wings spread wide, were hanging against the glass panes, caught by the condensation on the glass. It seemed to show that, at least in captivity, light forces are more attractive to insects than an abundant food supply. Each following morning the same scene repeated itself, until all the beetles had finally vanished, some of them escaping through the ventilation during daytime. The aphid population seemed unchanged.

Was this a valid experiment? If it had been repeated, would the outcome have been the same? I personally felt irresponsible and guilty enough not to launch a second trial. As a result, my attitude towards printed information regarding biological insect control in greenhouses is one of extreme caution. Human manipulation within the insect world has enormous consequences and in reality the outcome or result can hardly be predicted. Since the projected process is entirely based on natural science, and excludes even the smallest grain of spiritual understanding, the biodynamic grower will in each case have to exercise his most mature judgment in deciding to employ biological insect control in the greenhouse. Accepting responsibility for *all* life spheres does not make the choice easy.

CHAPTER 15

Plant Diseases

Those people who have occupied their minds and hands with biodynamic theory and practice for some time know of the unique statement which Rudolf Steiner made decades ago: The plant by its own nature cannot be diseased! It is the physical expression of the etheric world and as such derives its existence and continued support from the fountain of life itself. Disease originates from another realm, and the reasons for the development of disease have to be searched for there, not in the plant. Steiner's statement might be taken by some as a great relief, and yet the comprehension of the statement, and the personal confrontation with plant diseases — which by observation and experience are simply part of reality — are entirely different matters.

Again, in orthodox horticulture the greenhouse manager merely finds out what to spray. But what is the biodynamic grower supposed to do? Characteristically for bio-

97

dynamics, the answer does not lie in the formulation of a recipe for the prescribed sequence of a number of steps, but instead in the attempt to describe the interrelationships between the realms of nature involved. Out of this depth of understanding, the grower has to decide on the course of action to be taken should plant diseases become a problem. As in all spheres of life, emphasis needs to be placed upon prevention.

In accepting the premise that plants by their own nature cannot harbor the cause for disease, where must we look? The biodynamic approach to plant studies points to the environment of the plants, near and far. If there is any difficulty at all in comprehending this line of thought, more in-depth understanding of biodynamic/anthroposophical philosophy should be gained. Unfortunately, the scope of the specific subject area discussed in this text does not really allow me to elaborate on the broad range of philosophical ideas. Fortunately, on the other hand, such material is easily available for the serious student.

The environment of the plant is made up of spheres below and above ground; in other words, soil and micro- as well as macro-climate constitute the environment. In the greenhouse the soil area is scaled down to observable size, while the micro-climate can actually be controlled by the grower. The additional environment is the greenhouse itself. I have already stressed the importance of sanitation. One key to the prevention of plant diseases is right there! It is impossible to place too much emphasis on this one factor. Watering, and its proper handling in order to prevent plant disease, has also been discussed earlier. The water needs to be neutral, and the water temperature should *never* be lower than air temperature. A water heater is a necessity for biodynamic greenhouse management! Plant nutrition for greenhouse crops is of more decisive importance than for outdoor crops. Soil tests of potting soils and all other greenhouse soils are imperative. The availability of nutrients, the pH factor, and the organic matter content need to be known so as to project and predict plant performance. A weakened, under-nourished plant is more vulnerable to plant disease than a well-fed specimen. Greenhouse temperature has to be adjusted to the specific crop(s) grown. Night temperature is best set to be 10°F. lower than the day temperature on a cloudy day. Annual vegetable crops should be timed in such a way as to avoid the mid-winter season. Do not seed before the winter solstice.

Once all these considerations are taken into account, the only task is for me to emphasize again the importance of setting up a routine spraying program utilizing natural substances that support the life forces of the plant. Prevention is better than cure. Through proper greenhouse management, plant disease can for the most part be avoided.

CHAPTER 16

The Greenhouse Grower

The one most important factor for successful bio-dynamic greenhouse management is, of course, the person in charge, the grower. This is true for any type or method of greenhouse operation, but particularly so for the bio-dynamic approach. The greenhouse interior is an artificial environment entirely dependent upon the input of human effort and labor. The greenhouse is a human creation and only functional if taken care of by one. Have you ever seen a greenhouse which has been left unattended for a month? It is a far more desolate sight than an untended area in nature. There can be beauty in the desert and order in the jungle, but a greenhouse deserted by man/woman tells of death and treason.

There weaves a certain type of mutual sensitivity be-tween the relationship of greenhouse and grower. One could say that all elements in nature differ from each other by their degree of consciousness. The mineral has attained the least degree of consciousness, and the human being the highest here on earth. It is therefore the human being who can develop the highest form of awareness in regard to the other realms of nature. Spirituality is common to all realms. The task of the human being, as part of and in relation to nature, is to establish a link between the spirit of the human being and the spirit of nature. The greenhouse grower is no exception. For some, establishing such a relationship in the greenhouse might be harder than in the field and woods; for others, however, there might be no difference, or the path might even be easier. Experiences earlier in life, or at least the strong conviction of the reality of spirit existence, certainly are aids along the road.

I wish to emphasize the presence and importance of what is generally called the human attitude — in this case the attitude of the grower to the work and the living beings he deals with. This human attitude has a great deal of influence upon the outcome of every aspect of greenhouse work: seeding, making cuttings, transplanting, etc. Folklore or tradition said that people with a positive attitude towards the world of plants had a green thumb. In reality the thumb is dirty, but the color of the human spiritual attitude establishes a link to the physical green shades of plant life. These intangible, mysterious connections are realities which exist, whether or not they are rejected or accepted by the individual.

Quite often, during the course of training newcomers in greenhouse work, I have observed how people handle the job of making cuttings, of rosemary most often in our case. What is the mood of soul? How is the concentration? The technique is rather simple, the growing medium and greenhouse environment always uniform, but the mood of soul of the individual is different. Whenever the rate of success for the cuttings forming roots was low, there was usually a lack of self-assurance, of nervous uncertainty, lack of relaxation, lack of concentration. The desirable mood in dealing intimately with plants should be one which resembles meditation. The fortunate fact is that everyone can learn and acquire such a mood. The biodynamic greenhouse grower needs it more than anyone else.

CHAPTER 17

Conclusion

Where do we go from here? Into the future, no doubt, hopefully with progressive thoughts and noble deeds. The fact may not have occurred to anyone in biodynamic greenhouse growing that we as growers have made and still make use of technology which never even heard of nor made any use of biodynamic ideas. From greenhouse structure to heating systems, we use what is available, conceived and executed by the laws of material science alone. The denial of the spirit is, in a certain way, built into these contraptions and has to be conquered and overcome, or at least neutralized by the spirit nature of the biodynamic grower.

Will the day come when a spiritualized science will join with the efforts of the grower? At present, the food crops produced by the growers of the world are, in the broadest sense, lacking the forces desired by the human spirit. Emphasis on the physical appearance seems to overshadow all other considerations. May the future provide the light we all need to discover the proper way of producing and finding nourishment for both, the human body and the human spirit.